TOMMY JOHNSTON

—THE HAPPY WANDERER—

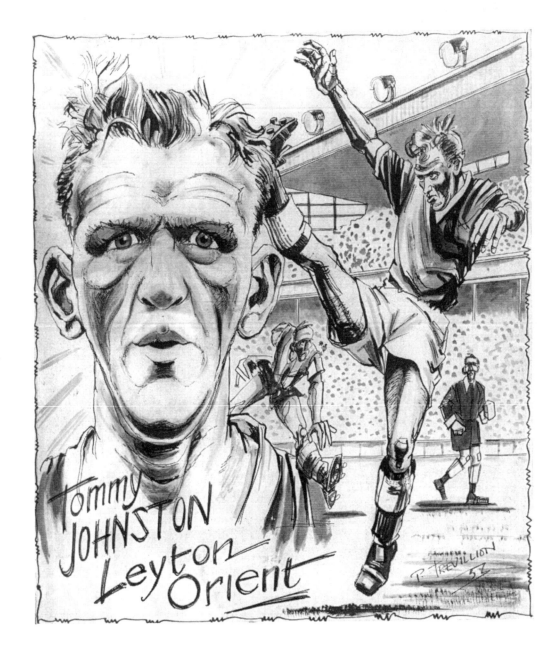

TOMMY JOHNSTON
—*THE HAPPY WANDERER*—

Neilson N. Kaufman
Assisted by Alan E. Ravenhill

'...the craggy Scot who finds it easier to score great goals than to talk about them; the soft-spoken leader who hits the ball as though he loathes leather and is always, in everything, so good.'

breedon **books**
PUBLISHING

First published in Great Britain by
The Breedon Books Publishing Company Limited
Unit 3, The Parker Centre, Mansfield Road, Derby, DE21 4SZ
2004.

ISBN 1 85983 432 9

Printed and bound by Cromwell Press, Trowbridge, Wiltshire

Contents

Acknowledgements

First and foremost, I would like to thank All Mighty God for allowing me good health and many happy days over this period of my life and for giving me the opportunity to work on this book with Alan Ravenhill. Thank you also to Jean and Tommy Johnston, their daughter Alison and their son Neil. Without the many emails, letters and photographs sent to me over the past year this book would not have been possible.

I would also like to thank my wife Debbie and twin daughters Amy and Samantha for their patience, love, support and prayers while I was working on this book.

Thanks also to both Jean and Tommy for sharing with the readers and myself their personal and many private thoughts and memories of past years. Also, thanks for all their time and effort in preparing and sending two audio tapes to me in South Africa. Also for all the checking of the various drafts of this book to ensure accuracy and for the opportunity to become good friends with them both and also with their children Alison and Neil.

To the others who have been a tremendous help in the compilation of this book, a very special thank you from the authors: David Adams, Anthony Ambrosen, Tony Brown, Sheila M. Millar, Andy Porter, David Ross, Steve Whitlam and Gerry Wolstenholme.

The authors would also like to thank the following people and organisations that have given their time generously: Donald Bell, Peter Chapman, Mike Childs, Mike Cork, Jim Creasy, Mike Davies, Bill Donnachie, Bob Dunning, Folkestone Library, Terry Frost, Joe Gilhooley, Michael Grade, Colin Hargreaves, Jack Huckel, Robert Illingworth, Steve Jenkins, Alison Bull (née Johnston), Emma Johnston, Jean Johnston, Neil Johnston, Derek Jones, Loanhead Library, Andy Mitchell, Richard Murrill, Donald Nannstead, *Peeblesshire News*, Matthew Porter, James M. Ross, Lola, Paolo and Gianni Sciacca, Scottish Football Association, Gareth Smith, Martin P. Smith, Karel J. Stokkermans, Roger J. Triggs, Leo Tyrie, Keith Warsop, Jim Younger and Delia Zussman.

The above names are listed in alphabetical order. Our sincere apologies to anyone who has mistakenly been left out.

The authors would also like to thank the following football clubs for their assistance: Blackburn Rovers, Blackpool, Crystal Palace, Darlington, East Stirlingshire, Folkestone Invicta, Gillingham, Glasgow Celtic, Glasgow Rangers, Kilmarnock, Leyton Orient, Norwich City, Oldham Athletic and Peebles Rovers.

Neilson N. Kaufman
Johannesburg, South Africa
September, 2004

Photograph credits

The authors have used a number of their own photographs for this book, but they would also like to thank Jean and Tommy Johnston for allowing the reproduction of many of the photographs used, which were from their own personal collection. In addition, a big thank you to Alison Bull (née Johnston) for her scanning and editing and the sending of many photographs to me via email, which really bring to life Tommy and Jean's stories of the past.

Steve Jenkins
The photograph of the Tommy Johnston Bar located at the East Stand north side at Brisbane Road, the home of Leyton Orient Football Club, is reproduced by courtesy of Steve Jenkins, deputy chairman of the Leyton Orient Supporters' Club.

Bob Stiggins
Thank you also to Bob Stiggins, photographer of the now defunct *News Chronicle* newspaper for taking some wonderful rapid-sequence photographs of Tommy scoring two goals against Grimsby Town in December 1957.

Paul Trevillion
Last but certainly not least, a big thank you to the highly acclaimed sports artist Paul Trevillion. He is known as the finest that Europe has ever produced and his work has taken him all over the world. Thank you again for allowing the reproduction in this book of your excellent caricature of Tommy Johnston from April 1957, which was presented to Tommy all those years ago.

Foreword

by Phil Woosnam

It was early in 1955, when stationed at Woolwich in south-east London for the remaining 18 months of my National Service, that I signed as an amateur for Leyton Orient.

At that time, the O's played in Division Three South. Manager Alec Stock and trainer Les Gore had previously demonstrated their strong belief that amateur players in their early twenties could step up to be as successful as professional players.

This somewhat unique philosophy, which contrasted with the highly successful 'Busby Babes' programme at Manchester United, would be further justified by the high standard achieved by former amateurs like Ken Facey, Vic Groves, Sid Bishop, Phil White, Len Julians, Ron Heckman and other teammates at the O's.

After a few weeks in the reserve team, being coached by Joe Mallett on the finer points of playing in midfield in a professional team, I made it to the first team to play alongside Tommy Johnston. Because of his experience, we quickly established an apparent telepathic understanding as we helped the O's gain promotion to Division Two. That understanding was probably a significant factor in both of us being transferred to Division One clubs – Tommy to Blackburn Rovers and me to West Ham United.

Although I was subsequently fortunate to develop a similar understanding with Vic Keeble, Johnny Dick and Geoff Hurst at Upton Park (and later with Derek Dougan and Tony Hateley at Aston Villa) nothing surpassed my experience of playing alongside Tommy Johnston as a regular first-team player at the O's.

Since those stimulating days at Brisbane Road and later with other clubs, Tommy and I have moved on to enjoy our lives in Australia and the United States respectively.

Could I have overcome the various twists and turns I have since encountered without benefiting from the experience, expertise and influence of Alec Stock, Les Gore, Joe Mallett and Tommy Johnston? I doubt it and now, some 50 years or so later, I welcome the opportunity to express my appreciation and best wishes to Tommy in this book about his amazing life story.

Yes, they were golden days we enjoyed together with our teammates at Leyton Orient.

Authors' Note: Phil Woosnam, the 'Welsh Wizard', was born in Caersws, a small Welsh village in Montgomeryshire, on 22 December 1932. He played for Wales as a schoolboy and youth international while attending Newtown Grammar School. Phil then spent four years at the University of Wales in Bangor, graduating with degrees in Physics and Mathematics, and making eight of his ultimate 15 appearances for the Welsh Amateur team. While at university, he also played for Manchester City as an amateur, making one League appearance.

He joined Leyton Orient on amateur forms in January 1955 and, after completing his National Service, took up a science teaching post at Leyton County High School. He starred in the O's 1955–56 championship season and in October 1958 he gained his first of 17 full caps for Wales. After playing 112 senior games, with 19 goals for the O's, he was transferred to West Ham United in November 1958 for a fee of £30,000. He stayed at Upton Park for four years, scoring 29 goals from 153 senior appearances, before joining Aston Villa for £27,000 in November 1962.

In August 1966, after playing 111 League games and scoring a further 29 goals for Villa, he emigrated to America to became a highly successful coach and manager with Atlanta Chiefs. He then served as commissioner of the North American Soccer League and vice-president of the United States Soccer Federation from 1969 to 1983.

Woosnam has perhaps done more than anyone else to bring the game of soccer to the United States, which culminated in the World Cup Finals being hosted very successfully there during 1994. In 1996, Woosnam managed the soccer semi-finals and finals for both men and women at the Olympic Games held in Atlanta, Georgia, US. In June 1997, he was inducted into the US National Soccer Hall of Fame in Oneonta, New York, having already been inducted into the Georgia Soccer Hall of Fame the previous January. Today Phil and his wife Ruth live in Atlanta.

Neil Kaufman is very happy to have Phil Woosnam write the foreword to this book, as Phil and Tommy were his favourite players when he was a young lad. But the last word on Phil Woosnam comes from Tommy Johnston himself, who said: 'Phil is the best player I have seen and ever played with and I feel honoured that he has written the foreword to this book on my life'.

Introduction

This book has been written as a belated attempt to do justice to a footballer who, although recognised as a good player, was never ranked as highly as he should have been. He was denied international recognition and that in itself was a mistake. The England manager at the time, Walter Winterbottom, gave Johnston this accolade: 'If Tommy Johnston was an Englishman, he would have been in my squad for the 1958 World Cup Finals in Sweden'.

But there is a lot more to Tommy Johnston than just football. Having been born in a small Scottish mining village called Loanhead in Midlothian, as a young man he was blighted at only 17½ by a terrible mining accident, which nearly cost him his arm. It kept him out of work and football action for over two years, but he gamely fought back to achieve a superb record in the game of football. He was voted Leyton Orient's greatest-ever player in a millennium poll of the club's supporters, and a Norwich newspaper also paid tribute to him as one of Norwich City's best-ever players.

This book is a tribute to Tommy Johnston. It not only takes a look at his life through his own eyes, but also includes the memories of his life and career of his wife Jean and children Alison and Neil. There is also plenty of comment and, for the first time, a full statistical record of his playing career, compiled by the authors.

It is the very first time that Tommy has spoken in such depth about his life as a boy, his mining accident and his 15 years in football. He is a shy and modest man, and he might wonder why there is all this fuss about him after all this time. The answer is that we feel that it is time to set the record straight: his achievements as a player ought to be seen in their proper context, up there with the very best.

Tommy was denied the international cap he so richly deserved – and that, sadly, cannot now be put right. But a proper examination of his career is long overdue.

Tommy Johnston, who stood 5ft 11¾in and weighed 12st 4lb during his playing days, was compared during his career to a number of the greatest-ever football players, including: Dixie Dean; Nandor Hidegkuti, the great Hungarian centre-forward; Tommy Lawton; Jimmy McGrory, still the record goalscorer from the Scottish League; and Arthur Rowley, who is still, to this day, the highest-ever goalscorer in English League football.

Tommy had some wonderful seasons with the likes of Kilmarnock, Norwich City, Newport County, Leyton Orient (twice), Blackburn Rovers and Gillingham. He ended his professional career with non-League Folkestone Town as player-coach, helping them reach the first round of the FA Cup, before bowing out from playing after a few games at Lytham St Annes. Then came his official retirement.

But just how good was Tommy Johnston? Unofficial records show that approximately 38,000 players (of which approximately 8,000 are forwards), have played in the English Football League since League matches commenced in the 1888–89 season. Yet to this day only 52 known players have scored more English League goals than Johnston's total of 239. He is also ranked joint 19th in the top seasonal all-time League goalscoring list on 43 goals. (A full breakdown of all these players appears at the end of Chapter 15.)

In the first edition of Barry Hugman's book *Rothmans Football League Player's Records*, published in 1981, the section covering 1946–75 listed 15,000 players. Of these, just 300 were profiled for their outstanding individual performances and Tommy Johnston was among them.

We, the authors, think his record speaks for itself, and that Tommy was clearly one of the great goalscorers and perhaps the greatest header of the ball in the history of the beautiful game. But we encourage you to read this account of Thomas Bourhill Johnston's life and playing record and make up your own mind.

The book is divided into two sections. The first is the story of Tommy Johnston's life as told to the authors, in his own words – and also a few from his family. In the second section the authors examine his career through statistics, reports in the press, fans' memories and other research.

Neilson N. Kaufman and Alan E. Ravenhill

Section One: Tommy in his own words

During the writing of this book Tommy Johnston has talked in detail to the authors about his life and his playing career. This is his story as he told it, in his own words.

Tommy Johnston's tale begins in Scotland, in the village of Loanhead in Midlothian, where he was born. It was made a Burgh of the Barony of Charles II on 14 May 1669. It is located five miles from Edinburgh, Scotland.

At the time of his birth in August 1927, it was a self-sufficient but poor community with local industry revolving around coal mining and shale. The population was just under 4,000 people. Loanhead was surrounded by hills, valleys and farmland. The housing and pits in the village were all privately owned by the Shotts Iron Company Ltd. The coal-mining industry is all gone now.

Valuable research by Sheila M. Millar of the Loanhead Library and local Loanhead historian David Adams shows that there have been a few famous people born in the mining village of Loanhead over the years. They include: Sir William McTaggart, a local artist; Josephine Purcell, a nun who provided homes for street children in Bolivia; Revd Joseph Hannan, one of the founders of Hibernian Football Club; Andrew Kennedy, East of Scotland snooker/billiard champion; and Helen Flockhart, captain of the Scotland ladies' hockey team. There are also some decent footballers, all born after Tommy, who made it into the English League.

Alex Young was born in Loanhead on 3 February 1937 and started with Hearts before moving south to join Everton in November 1960. He stayed for seven years at Goodison, making 228 League appearances and scoring 77 goals. After a spell with Glentoran, he joined Stockport County in November 1968 and played 23 games with them, netting five goals. He won eight full Scottish caps. Young also won English FA Cup medals, an English League championship winners' medal, Scottish League, Scottish Cup and Scottish League Cup medals.

John Ian Aitken King was born in Loanhead on 27 May 1937 and was a Scottish schoolboy international centre-half, who started off with Arniston Rangers, but it was while with Leicester City that he made his name. He arrived at Filbert Street in June 1957 and made 224 League appearances, scoring six goals. He moved to Charlton Athletic in March 1966, making 63 League appearances.

James Steele, born in Loanhead on 11 March 1950, was a centre-half who started off with Dundee, before moving south to join Southampton in January 1972. He stayed for four years and made 161 League appearances, and won an English FA Cup-winners' medal with the Saints when they beat Manchester United 1–0 in 1976.

Gary Andrew Naysmith is the latest and possibly the most successful of the Loanhead-born players at international level (along with Alex Young). Born in Loanhead on 16 November 1979, the defender started off with Whitehill Welfare Colliery before moving to Hearts in June 1996. He made 92 (4) Scottish League appearances, with three goals, before a £1.75 million move south to join Everton. At the time of writing, Naysmith has made 93 (12) League appearances for the Toffees, with five goals. He had also won 21 Scottish caps, the most recent, in a 0–0 draw with Slovenia in a World Cup qualifier.

Chapter 1

Loanhead and the early years

Tommy's dedication

I would like to thank my brothers for maintaining my interest in football and my family for their encouragement after the mining accident to get back into the game when my confidence was at a low ebb.

Also my wife Jean and children Alison and Neil for traipsing around the country for over 12 years, while I followed my dream.

Tommy Johnston
January 2004

I was born on Thursday 18 August 1927. My parents were Robert or Bob Johnston, as he was always known, who was born in Straiton, Midlothian, and Margaret Nelson, known as Meg, who was a local Loanhead lass. My birth took place at our home, 7 Ramsey Square, on one of the oldest streets in Loanhead village. At the time the property was valued at £7 0s 5d; my Father paid a rateable value of seven shillings per year. Our house was a small two-bedroomed cottage with a front room.

EXTRACT ENTRY OF BIRTH: 17 & 18 Victoriæ Cap. 80, § 37.

No.	Name and Surname.	When and Where Born.	Sex.	Name, Surname, and Rank or Profession of Father. Name, and Maiden Surname of Mother. Date and Place of Marriage.	Signature and Qualification of Informant, and Residence, if out of the House in which the Birth occurred.	When and Where Registered, and Signature of Registrar.
140	Thomas Bourhill Johnston	1927. August Eighteenth 6h 40 A.M. 7 Ramsay Square Loanhead	M	Robert Johnston Coalminer Margaret Nelson Johnston M S Bourhill 1920 April 15th Edinburgh	(Signed) Robert Johnston Father Present	1927. August 21st At LASSWADE (Signed) James Robt Registrar

TRACTED from the REGISTER BOOK OF BIRTHS, for the PARISH of LASSWADE in the COUNTY of MIDLOTHIAN, this Twenty-first day of August Nineteen Hundred and Twenty Seven. Patrick Goldie Asst Registrar.

I was born with green eyes and was christened Thomas Bourhill Johnston (Bourhill being my mother's maiden name) at the Church of Scotland. I soon became known as Tommy. When I was born, I had a sister, May McIntosh, who was nine years old and four brothers, Robert (seven years old), Alexander (five), Harry (four) and James (two). In 1930 my sister Margaret was born and two years later along came brother Archibald, the last of the Johnston clan.

By 2004, Harry had died. May McIntosh is now 85 and Robert is 83 (they are both in care), James is 78, I'm 76, then Margaret is 73 and Archie is 71.

May McIntosh is my half-sister; my mother was divorced when she met my father. May was her daughter by her first husband, whom it is believed was killed in World War One.

Once I got a bit older, I moved with my brothers into the front room of the house. My mother and father had one bedroom and sister Margaret the other. I remember my brothers' beds in the house were fitted into two recesses in the front room: three of the boys had beds in one recess and the older two boys in the other. When the beds were folded back into the wall recesses, it gave us a lot more space.

As a wee lad, I often played football on a small field across the road from my house in Ramsey Square and on Saturdays I went to watch whippet racing there. The football field had a long history, and was used as far back as 1883 by local football teams like Benburb, Mayflower and Poulton Vale.

A year after my sister Margaret was born, in December 1931, the family moved into a larger house, just up the road at No.3 Goldie Terrace (although the house still stands in 2004, the street was renamed many years ago and is now McKinley Terrace). We moved at the right time as, two years later, houses 1–20 in Ramsey Square were demolished by the local council, which stated that these 20 houses had become unfit for human habitation and could not be rendered fit at reasonable expense.

Our new house was known as a five-ender: it had four bedrooms, a front room, a kitchen and a bathroom. This was the first time that the family had had access to a bathroom. Even the local mine had no bathing facilities until 1931, when water was first provided for the local pithead and baths made available for the miners.

In 1933 I first attended Loanhead Infants School. My Dad, who worked down the local coal pit, was the only breadwinner, so money was always short. I never had a pair of shoes to wear to infants school – I went with bare feet.

I enjoyed playing football in the street as a wee young lad – we used a small ball because it was easier to kick around without shoes. The lads called it the 'wee tanner ball', it was like a tennis ball and all the kids took one to school and we kicked them about in the yard, trying to impress each other with our skill.

As the kids grew up in Loanhead, most of the recreational activities were 'anything that was free' such as picnics in the woods and swimming in the pit water-hole, which was clean, except at the bottom, and playing and talking football with friends. We also enjoyed, if we were given any pocket money, going to the local picture house.

Pentland Hills was a well-known beauty spot, approximately three miles from Loanhead, where my brothers, friends and I spent time during weekends and holidays enjoying a picnic and playing, chasing and hopefully catching rabbits to put some food on the table. I enjoyed camping and hiking too. We also cycled to Portobello, near Edinburgh, to the swimming pool. It had a great feature, I think it was the first ever pool in the UK to have artificial waves. During the summer holidays, we would go to Glasgow to visit the 'Barras' market – and visiting the famous castle in Edinburgh was always enjoyable. Television was not available then and played no part in our lives. (The first television I ever saw was when living in Newport during the 1954–55 season.)

My memories of Loanhead are still very clear. I can remember the buildings, the businesses and the local cinema, owned by a Mr Brodie, but especially Alfonzo Forte's Ice Cream Parlour in the High Street, which also had a billiard room. The Forte family in later years went on to build the famous Forte Hotel chain.

As I was growing older, my schooling took place at Loanhead Primary and then I attended the Loanhead Public School. It was not to my liking and I had very little interest in learning apart from playing sport, although I did enjoy some geography and maths (definitely not algebra). I hated exams, and all of us wee lads knew we would finish up in the local coal pit, so what was the point of studying? I would rather play a game of football.

At the age of 10, I was picked to play for the school team at outside-left, even though you weren't supposed to play for a school team until you were 11. All the lads in the team pleaded with the teacher, Mr Trail, to pick me for the replay of a final. After much consideration, he dropped the lad who had played left wing and had not been up to standard, and put me in the team.

My footballing talent is first spotted

I owe a big thank you to Mr Chris Bell, the school janitor, who was a well-known personality in Midlothian school sporting circles. He was the one who first spotted that I might have some talent. He taught me a lot out in the playground.

Old Mr Bell was not a local. I was told he was actually born in Scarborough, but after moving to Loanhead he lived at 25 Kennington Avenue. He taught me another thing, not only for playing football but also for my daily living: if you do something and if you keep practising all the time you can achieve anything. I always remembered those words and I practised the art of heading a ball from a jumping and standing position on a daily basis.

To this day I always think of what old Mr Bell taught me, and it helped me progress to Loanhead Mayflower, Peebles Rovers, Kilmarnock and finally down to England. When I was with them, I was kicking a ball harder with my left foot than with my natural right and my heading from all different angles had become very natural, but I still practised and practised every day on my own.

In the days before I played football seriously I couldn't kick a ball with my left foot and it was Mr Bell who took me under his wing. I went with him out on the field every afternoon for a few weeks and he showed me how to kick with my left, how to take corner kicks and pass and head the ball and that was my first experience of someone coaching me.

> *Mr Bell's son Donald kindly supplied the following about his father in 2004:*
>
> *My father was born in Scarborough, Yorkshire in 1893. He went to sea with the Booth Line out of Liverpool when aged 15. Subsequently, he joined the Royal Navy and spent 22 years in that service, taking part in the Battle of Jutland and fighting at the Dardanelles in World War One. He married my mother, Annie Jane Reid from Newtongrange, in 1920, and they had three children: Doreen, who worked in William Jack chemist's shop, younger brother Ronnie and myself. On retirement he was, for a short time, caretaker of the Miners Institute before becoming the janitor of the Loanhead Public School, where he remained until his retirement aged 65. He died in 1988, aged 95.*

From then on it was my oldest brother Robert, who was on the books of Falkirk at the time, who coached me. We would play head tennis with a 'shilling ball', which was a size-four ball made of rubber. I loved heading it from all different angles and getting it between two sticks that acted as goalposts. Robert bought me my first pair of football boots to play in my first big game for the school team and that was it – the start of my career as Tommy Johnston the footballer. At the age of 10 I was very proud to be carrying on in the Johnston tradition of playing football. I know my family thought I was a good player, but they had no idea then what would happen in the future.

Our school team, Loanhead Bluebell, drew 2–2 with Newbattle in the final of the Midlothian Schools Cup. I played at outside-left in the replay, which was held on the Bonnyrigg Rose Athletic ground and I scored two headed goals in a 4–2 victory. From then on I was always in the school team. At 13, I captained the school team in the mornings and played for the under-17 side, which was called Loanhead West End, in the afternoon – but it was only recreation for me at that time.

I was very happy when I left school in June 1941. I was nearly 14 years old and it was time to say goodbye to the headmaster, Mr David McNeil, and my teacher, Ms Sutherland. I then fulfilled one of my great ambitions (the other, of course, being playing football) when I started work at the mine after a few months of summer holidays. I officially joined the pit just after my 14th birthday, in August 1941.

I remember my parents buying my pit clothing and carbine lamp so that I would be ready to go underground. On my first day at the pit I was met by my Uncle Jim, who was a foreman. He put me to work on the tumbler, which was to do with loosening the hutches and emptying out the coal into a pile.

I stayed one year on the surface and then I went underground and worked as a clipper, and thought it was the cat's whiskers. I thought I was so grown up, working with my father and brothers and earning my first wage of £2 10s a week. The financial burdens on the family had eased a little now that me and all my older brothers were at the mine and earning a wage.

Working down the mine was always a tough job: the miners worked very hard for their money. I used to start at 7am and finish around 2.30pm. Quite often the hutches went off the rails with a ton of coal in them. They had to be lifted back onto the rails, and the youngsters were the ones that did all this type of work. It was always so dark down there, although sometimes you could see the light from a colleague's carbine lamp. In later years they changed to electric lamps, but in the old days if your flint in your lamp went out for any reason, you were anchored – you couldn't go anywhere because it was just too dark. It was frightening, and for a young lad it wasn't an easy life being down a coal mine.

At the age of 16 I was still playing for the juvenile side Loanhead West End in my spare time, although I wanted to progress and play football like my Dad and brothers (although the term 'junior or juvenile' bore no reference to age – in Scotland at the time the juvenile football was the grade below League 'B' football). My Dad told me he had played in local football as a left-half and in his day he was quite a decent amateur player. Robert, my oldest brother, played at left-half-back or centre-half for Loanhead Mayflower and was also a reserve player with Falkirk, although in later years he played for the first team in the War League.

Harry, a left-half, was also with Loanhead Mayflower and he was a Hibernian reserve-team player. Hibs had a strong first team in those days. My other brothers, Alex and Archie, were later both goalkeepers at junior level. The talk in the house was often about the fortunes of Heart of Midlothian and Glasgow Rangers, although Celtic was a no-no.

I seemed to lose interest in playing for a while in my late teens, but my career picked up again when I signed for local juvenile side Gilmerton Drumbirds (what names we had for our minor clubs in Scotland!) and I was still playing at inside-left. I hated that position, and I always wanted to play centre-forward like the Glasgow Rangers youngster Willie Thornton. I never really got into the game when I was stuck out on the wing and making goals for others.

Then came the day when the centre-forward failed to turn up for a match. I volunteered for the position and had a good game and apart from a few matches at inside-forward, I mostly stayed as a centre-forward until much later in my career. My game improved and I became a lot more enthusiastic about training.

My aspirations to play semi-professional football were dented when, at 17½ years old, a serious mining accident nearly cost me my arm. The accident happened just before noon on 17 February 1945 at the Burghlee pit (pronounced *bear-lee*), one of the coal pits owned by the Shott's Iron Company in the area, close to the Ramsey pit (Burghlee closed down in the 1960s).

I was doing my normal job of clipping – which is taking the empty hutches in and then taking the hutches full of coal out. The accident was partly my own fault. I tried to couple the hutches together without taking my time (hutches were made of wood, with iron axles and iron wheels for carting coal on tracks that run like a railway).

I was in too much of a hurry, and my left wrist got caught between two hutches. It was one of those almost daily mishaps in the quest for coal, nothing to warrant headlines, not even in the local newspaper.

I couldn't look down at my wrist, I was just in too much shock. I rushed out and showed David Doig, the safety officer. He didn't have a splint so he put a bandage on my mangled wrist then rolled up newspapers to act as a splint, to keep the wrist secure until I arrived at the Edinburgh Royal Infirmary.

Doig called for an ambulance and on the way to the hospital the ambulance driver stopped at my house to tell my mother about the accident. She stayed at home so she could tell the rest of the family and we carried on to the hospital. The surgeon professor at the Royal Infirmary examined me and said that my arm was too badly crushed to be saved – it would have to be amputated.

However, his assistant, a Mr Smith, asked the professor if he could have a go at saving the arm and he was quickly given permission. I spent many hours down in theatre while they took bits of splintered bone out and, when he had finished, I spent a few days there recovering. I was then taken to the Peel Hospital in Galashiels to see the finest bone specialist in the country, a Professor Pollack. In hindsight I owe a great deal to these two gentlemen, Mr Smith and Professor Pollack, for their care.

I was in and out of hospital for over two years having skin grafts and various treatments. They took a piece of skin off my stomach to put on my arm and then skin off my leg to put on my stomach. Eventually, the arm was fully repaired, although it had a distinct bend on the outer side of the wrist and it was also much bulkier. The arm never grew any more, and it caused me to be very self-conscious.

When I first started playing football again, I wore an aluminium splint over the wrist, but I was soon told it was too dangerous to be worn on the field of play.

That's when I first wore a bandage, which I put on myself for many years either at home or in the dressing room before football matches. It protected my arm while playing, and I arrived early on home match days and put a fresh bandage on at the ground. For away games I put the bandage on at home first.

During the two-year period after the accident, which was during World War Two, I had to stay at home because I was on compensation and was not allowed to work at the coal pit or to play any wartime football. It was a boring and very difficult time in my life, and it was also quite hard on my family. My boyhood dream of playing semi-professional football had been put on hold for the time being.

It upset me in later life to read an article by Basil Easterbrook that appeared in a football magazine during December 1958. The head-line stated that I had been half-killed under tons of rock and that I had sustained a broken leg in the mine accident. This article was pure journalistic sensationalism: the bit about being half-killed under tons of rubble was totally untrue and the story was not obtained from my family or myself. The real truth concerning the broken leg part of the story was as follows.

When I was on leave from Peel Hospital over a weekend, one of our neighbours bought a second-hand circular saw and a man was trying to get it started. We were all gathered around watching with interest. Then I heard a peculiar noise and I moved back, but the rest of the lads stood their ground.

The flywheel had broken and a small piece of it broke off and hit me straight on the leg, causing a fracture. I couldn't believe it! Here I was on leave recuperating from my arm injury, and I managed to get a broken leg as well. I was taken back to hospital. The doctor, who couldn't believe my bad luck, said it was a greenstick fracture.

That arm and the leg took a few months to come right and then I felt ready to return to the football field. I had no thought whatsoever of going back to pushing hutches down the pit.

Chapter 2

The start of a professional football career

After just over two years of being on compensation I was at last given the all-clear to play football again, and I still had the interest in it despite my long lay-off. I signed a short-term contract with Loanhead Mayflower during the first week of March 1947. They were a semi-professional juvenile outfit who had a number of former professional players in their ranks. The club colours at the time were blue and yellow shirts with white shorts.

Matches were played in Loanhead and not in the shadow of Scott's Monument in Princess Street, Edinburgh, as stated in some articles on my career over the years. Today Mayflower no longer exists. I was sad to be told that the club folded in 1964, having been in existence for over 80 years.

I earned 6s 6d per week as a part-time footballer, which I used as pocket money. Eventually I saved enough to be able to buy my own soccer boots. That's why many of the young miners who had some sort of ability also wanted to play football – to earn extra money to supplement their weekly mining income or to get away from the mine altogether.

My boyhood idol was the young Glasgow Rangers forward, Willie Thornton – I always wanted to play and head a ball like him. When I first started playing for the school team at 10 years of age, Thornton had just made his League debut for Rangers. He was just 16 years old and he went onto became one of their greatest-ever players. He was noted for his old-fashioned style of centre-forward play and for his great heading ability, winning seven caps for his country. In later years, he went into management before being appointed match-day host at the Thornton Suite at Ibrox; he died in August 1991.

I always practised heading a ball with my brothers, still using the rubber 'shilling ball' because it was all we could afford at the time. Heading was now becoming a big strength of mine. I remember the old saying 'practice makes perfect' and, in my case, this certainly proved to be true.

When I was 20, a scout asked my brother Harry if he knew of a decent centre-forward to play in a one-off match for Kelso United who were short of some players. He said 'I have a brother named Tommy who can play at centre-forward' – and so I went up with Harry, along with two other players from Loanhead Mayflower (Jimmy Mann and Jimmy Watson – neither of these lads made it into the big time) to play against a strong Hibernian 2nd XI.

Kelso won 3–1, and I scored a hat-trick in what turned out to be my only game for them. They wanted me to sign, but I said no. It was the only time the Hibs reserve side had been beaten all season. In goal for Hibs that day was my coal-mining buddy, Tommy Younger.

Tommy Younger

Tommy Younger was a good friend to me when we worked together down the coal pit, and he became a very good goalkeeper both for Hibs and down in England with Liverpool and Leeds United. He started with a juvenile team called Hutchinson Vale and we faced each other when I was with Loanhead Mayflower. Younger had decided to go into the mine rather than into the Army, and he worked alongside me.

I asked him what the most important thing to him about football was and he replied, 'These hands to keep out the English'. He eventually changed his mind about working in the pit and decided to go into the Army. He said 'I think I'll join the Army after all, it can't be worse than being down here'. He went to Edinburgh and gave himself up to the Military Police and joined the Army. After his training camp, he went over to Germany and Hibs flew him home every Friday so he could play for them. He won 24 caps for Scotland and played in the World Cup in Sweden during 1958.

In later years, when with he was Liverpool, I think he must have put the jinx on me. I didn't score many goals against him and even a good'un – a long header which flew past him from over 20 yards – was disallowed by the referee for offside, a decision that amazed me and most of the people at the ground.

I remember when Younger was player-manager with Falkirk, he brought his team down to Brisbane Road to play Leyton Orient in a friendly. I still didn't score against him or his side – we drew 2–2 – but after the match we went out for a few beers and we talked over all the memories of those early days. We chatted about playing against each other and the hard times being down the coal pit. In later life Younger was president of the Scottish FA for a time, but he was only 53 when he died on 13 January 1994, a few months after a heart operation.

The manager of Hibs at the time was Hughie Shaw and he asked Harry if I would come on trial with them. I thought long and hard about the offer, but I said no. The problem was that I was young, and I felt that if I joined a big club the players there would be far too good and I would never get a first-team game. I thought I should go to a smaller club where I could play regularly and move my way up. Looking back, maybe I was wrong in my thinking.

So instead, after leaving Loanhead Mayflower (I was with them just for a few months) my brother and I wanted to play at a higher level. We both went to talk to Peebles Rovers, who played in the East of Scotland League. At the time, I thought Harry was the best player in our family.

It was a good standard of football at Peebles, being one level below the 'C' Division of the Scottish League. Peebles Rovers were one of the oldest clubs in Scotland having been formed in 1884.

We travelled to their Whitestone Park Ground and were signed on for £2 per week in August 1947 by the man who ran the club, Jock Brown. At last I was picked in my favourite position, centre-forward, and I scored over 50 goals for the club. I can't remember the exact number but it was at least an average of two or three goals per match over the two good seasons I spent with the Rovers.

My football boot size as an adult was 7½, although my shoe size was a 9. The players had to get two sizes smaller to wear. We put on the boots and put our feet with the boots on into a bowl of water. This was done more than once to stretch the boots and mould them to the feet, and I lost both my big toenails because of this at the end of both seasons.

I started off well with Peebles, scoring a hat-trick at Coldstream in the first round of the Scottish Qualifying Cup. We then got thumped in the second round 7–1 at Edinburgh City, although I bagged our single goal. I thought I looked quite smart in a brand new kit: an all-red shirt with white shorts.

A man who had a big influence on me at Peebles Rovers was their player-manager Jerry Kerr, who was very knowledgeable about football. He taught me a lot, but then he left to manage Berwick Rangers. Kerr later managed Alloa Athletic and also spent more than 12 years as manager of Dundee United. He died in 1999.

An old Peebles Rovers fan was talking to Gareth Smith, the current secretary of the club, some 57 years later, in November 2003, in a Peebles pub. He said:

> *I remember a 22-year-old blonde-haired player named Tommy Johnston very well. He scored lots of goals for us and one in particular stands out for me, it was a remarkable goal he scored, when he returned a goal kick directly back into the net with a mighty powerful header*

*from around the halfway line. I could see this wee young
man had something special and it was no surprise when he
moved to a higher grade with Kilmarnock and later played
in England, I followed his career with great interest.*

The following season I netted five goals in the Scottish Cup.
During September 1948, in a first qualifying round tie, I scored two
goals against Babcock & Wilcox and in the second qualifying round
I got a hat-trick against the Duns Club.

Falkirk enquired about me and I went for a month's trial with
them. In one of the games I was up against Aberdeen's Kenny
Thomson. We were beaten 6–2, but I scored both goals. I later played
against him when he was with both Stoke City and Middlesbrough,
and I scored plenty against old Kenny.

Falkirk offered me a contract, but I turned it down, and because
of the trial I missed out on Peebles' third qualifying cup match. I was
really glad I hadn't been there because the lads were given a terrible
hiding at Forfar Athletic, losing 8–1. While I was away at Falkirk,
Peebles used a makeshift centre-forward named Ian Muir. He was
quite a useful defender, but he didn't do much good for them up front
at Forfar. Muir was born in Motherwell on 16 June 1929, had a few
seasons in the English League as a defender with both Bristol Rovers
and Oldham Athletic, and between 1953 and 1957 he made a total
of 61 career League appearances.

I remember very well two matches that I played in for Peebles
during September 1949. They were both in the first round of the
Scottish Qualifying Cup. The first was at East Stirlingshire and we
drew 3–3, and then we lost the replay at home to them 3–4. I bagged
two hat-tricks in these games. Their centre-half was Ralph Collins,
who was a professional player. He was so impressed by my ability as
a centre-forward and the fact that I scored six goals against him that
he recommended me to Kilmarnock, whose manager was Alex
Hastings. What I didn't know at the time was that Collins himself
was also about to sign for Kilmarnock.

Airdrie-born Collins joined Kilmarnock for £1,000 in October
1949 and he stayed for over 10 years, making 330 senior

appearances. He was later with Airdrie and was their manager between 1967–70 when he was surprisingly sacked after they had defeated Nottingham Forest on penalties in the inaugural Texaco Cup Final.

Proud to be a Killie player

Alex Hastings came through to Loanhead and we chatted for a wee while. I liked what he had to say, but in between his visits I had a brief trial with Third Lanark. Bolton Wanderers also offered me a month's trial but I refused, wanting to stay at home in Scotland. I was not ready to move south just yet.

Eventually, my decision was made and I contacted Hastings. He returned to see me in Loanhead and I signed for Kilmarnock in the Miners Welfare during November 1949. I was on a weekly wage of £6 (more than my father was earning for five days a week down the pit). The Miners Welfare was a hall where the miners could play snooker, dominoes and darts, and it also had an outside bowling green. It was paid for by the miners themselves; the Shotts Company deducted five pence per month from their pay.

A writer on Kilmarnock Football Club, David Ross, wrote in his book *Killie – the Official History*:

> *Manager Hastings pulled off two master strokes in 1949, with the signings of the big blonde centre-forward Tommy Johnston who joined from Peebles Rovers in November, who turned out to be a most prolific goalscorer and an excellent forward. He also signed defender Ralph Collins a month earlier, he would serve Killie superbly for more than 10 years.*

During 1950 I lived at the Wheatsheaf Hotel in Kilmarnock, along with players Jimmy Smith and Jackie Davidson, from Monday to Friday and went home after the match on Saturday. During my first few months with Killie, I worked at the ground with Jimmy Hood and two ground staff lads. We cleaned the stand after a home game and replaced the divots on the football field.

Young Jimmy Hood went onto have a long career with Killie

between 1945 and 1954, making 251 appearances and scoring 10 goals before moving on to coach Kilwinning Rangers. Jackie Davidson was an inside-forward who started with junior side Dundee Violet before joining Dundee United in June 1946. He was then with East Fife in 1947. He joined Killie for £1,500 in February 1950 but only played seven games, scoring once before joining Rhyl Athletic in October 1951. Jimmy Smith, a good friend of mine, was a reserve player who never made it in the Scottish League, although he continued his career in junior football.

Once I was chosen for the first team I was a bit apprehensive, but my second oldest brother, Alex, went with me to every Kilmarnock game to give me moral support. Everything went along fine at Killie and I really enjoyed working with Alex Hastings. I made my senior debut for them on 10 December 1949, against Hamilton Academical. I scored both goals in a 2–0 win and I felt good in the blue and white hooped shirt.

On 14 January 1950 we won at Queens Park 3–1. I scored our second goal in front of a record Scottish crowd for a match played outside the top division – 27,205 fans crowded into the ground. Queens Park's home ground was the famous Hampden Park and we were cheered on by more than 10,000 Killie fans.

On 4 March 1950 I was sent off for raising a foot on the goalkeeper during a 1–1 draw with Dumbarton. I didn't think it was that bad but I was suspended for a week. At least I scored our goal.

During April the club arranged three home friendly games. In the first we beat Buckie Thistle 2–1 and I scored one of the goals. Then came my first taste of playing against the English. We entertained English First Division side Derby County and got thrashed 1–5. County had a number of international players on the pitch, including Peter Doherty, Horatio 'Raich' Carter and Jack Stamp. The match was arranged as part of the deal that took Hugh McLaren to Derby, and over 17,900 people turned up for the match. On 22 April 1950, Irish side Derry City were the visitors to Rugby Park and I bagged five goals – all headers – in our 10–3 win. Our forward line was: McKay, McGill, Johnston, McDowell and Donaldson and we certainly turned it on that day. They were a good bunch of lads and, like me, both McDowell and McKay ended up playing in the English League.

The following month we went to Peebles Rovers for a friendly as part of my transfer deal, so the home side could make some gate money. We drew 1–1.

I ended my first season in senior football with 15 League and Cup goals from 19 appearances, which made me the club's top goalscorer. We were a well-supported club – the best in 'B' Division – with an average home crowd of over 10,300, yet despite the boom the club was actually losing money.

Malky MacDonald – not my cup of tea

Sadly, Hastings left Killie in April 1950. The following month I played in the semi-final of the 'B' Division Supplementary Cup (this competition was like today's LDV Vans Trophy) against St John-stone, and I scored in our 2–2 draw. The following season I missed the second leg, which Killie won 2–0, but somehow the final was never played. It would have would been nice to have won a medal.

The man to replace Hastings was the former Celtic man Malcolm 'Malky' MacDonald, who took over the reins having joined us from Brentford. I found him a strange man. He just wouldn't let you forget that he was a former Glasgow Celtic player and that they had beaten Everton in the final of the Empire Exhibition Trophy played at Ibrox in 1938, and he kept on and on about his former Celtic days. One day I said to him 'Are you actually interested in Kilmarnock, all you talk about is Celtic!'. I could not stand the man and his bloody Celtic. He got through to me so much that even today I can still name the Celtic team that won that cup off by heart.

Thinking back, I suppose MacDonald did care about Killie. He had two further spells as their boss in the 1950–57 and 1965–67 seasons. Under his leadership the team gained promotion from the 'B' Division in 1954, and got into a League Cup Final and the Scottish Cup Final in 1957, although the club lost both these finals. In 1957 he returned to Brentford and took them to the Fourth Division championship and he was also caretaker manager of Scotland for a short time.

I'm told that throughout MacDonald's many years with Killie he never once had a contract. For all his success, he was not my cup of tea. I preferred the way things were under Alex Hastings – for me that was great, he was a very good man.

Born in Falkirk on 26 October 1913, Alexander Cockburn Hastings was also a fine left-half with Stenhousemuir. He played for Sunderland between August 1930 and 1945, making a total of 266 League appearances and scoring four goals. He won two Scottish caps in 1936 and 1938 and a Football League Championship medal in 1936. He then joined Kilmarnock as manager, and it was the only club he ever managed.

I remember a League match at Ayr United in August 1950. We had kicked off, but then all the players heard a rumpus and stopped playing. Hundreds of our fans, who were still waiting to get in, lifted one of the entrance gates off its hinges and swarmed into the ground free of charge. They would certainly have missed a good game if they had remained outside. For once I didn't score, but we drew 2–2.

The following season started off alright for me at Killie with a League Cup goal against Dunfermline Athletic. However, there was one match I would rather forget. It was on 27 January 1951, a Scottish Cup match against 'C' Division side East Stirlingshire, one division below us. I personally had a good game and made a goal three minutes into the second half for our right winger McKay, but they knocked us out 2–1. It was very embarrassing for us because earlier in the season our reserve side had beaten them easily.

As time went on I got so fed up with Mr MacDonald that I asked to leave in February 1951. He did not pick me again and they eventually gave me a free transfer the following April. It proved to be Killie's worst season for many a year, as they finished 12th out of 16 in the 'B' Division. I played my last game for them on 3 February 1951, scoring at Dunfermline. My Killie career ended with 20 goals from 27 appearances.

The local newspaper wrote that they were disappointed that I was leaving:

We are most disappointed that Killie have not attempted to retain the services of Tommy Johnston for the 1951–52 season. He was in such great form up to being left out of the team by manager MacDonald. His play was always a feature of Killie matches and most of the beleaguered pivots reflected afterwards that they would rather have him [Johnston] in their side than have to play against him. A feature of his great play is that he can head a ball with a power that many players find difficult to match with a shot.

I will always remember the advice I got from the veteran and former Third Lanark, Kilmarnock and East Stirlingshire player Johnny Kelly when he was at Killie. He told me:

Whatever you do son, don't stay with one club for long, you must get about a bit. Don't be a fool like me, nine years with one club, then kicked out on a free transfer before we could discuss any benefit match.

Full-back Johnny Kelly had joined Third Lanark from Scottish junior football in August 1941 and spent nine years with Thirds before being given a free transfer. In 1947 he appeared for the Scottish League versus the English League and was given a hard time by Stanley Matthews. He joined Kilmarnock in June 1950, receiving not even a thank you letter from his previous club. This could be the reason why a number of the older players dashed off in 1950 to play in Columbia, risking a lifetime ban when they returned to Scotland. Kelly ended his career with East Stirling in 1954.

Benefit matches for players in Scotland were a contentious issue at the time and it was only in the 1951–52 season that Robert 'Bob' Thyne, the man who recommended me to Darlington, was the first Killie player to win a benefit in over 20 years.

Talking of benefits, Jimmy Kelly also told me about a player named Jimmy Middlemass, who was a good player for junior side Petershill and stayed with them right up to the age of 29. It was only in 1949 that he decided to turn professional with Kilmarnock. He earned more money in junior football where there was no capping of wages and they gave players benefits for long service, which didn't happen with a League club. That's why good players often stayed with a junior side, because of the benefit issue. The lure of the professional game finally became too much for Middlemass, and he turned to the pro game very late on in his career – for the experience rather than the money.

Chapter 3

Down to England

After leaving Kilmarnock in April 1951, I went home and worked as a labourer at the pit in Loanhead for a short spell. Then Glasgow-born Bob Thyne, the former Clydebank centre-half who was a Killie player at the time, liked the way I played and was often complimentary about my heading ability. He recommended me to the Darlington boss George Irwin. Thyne had played a number of wartime games for Killie, and in 1946 he also played in seven League games for Darlington.

Born in Smethwick, Birmingham, George Irwin joined West Bromwich Albion as a goalkeeper but did not appear in the first team. He arrived at Crystal Palace in 1921, then had a three-year spell with Reading before being appointed coach to Southend United. He was promoted to assistant manager, then became a coach at Sheffield Wednesday and was on their staff when the Owls won the FA Cup in 1935. He returned to Palace as coach and then assistant manager in July 1939 and stayed until May 1947, when he took up a role as a scout. He was appointed Darlington boss in April 1950 and stayed at Feethams for two seasons.

Joining Darlington

Bob Thyne was a good man and he kindly sent a letter telling Irwin all about me. Irwin must have liked what he read because he travelled up to Loanhead to chat with me and discuss the possibility of me playing in England. I was impressed by what he had to say and he offered me a whopping £14 per week plus bonuses which seemed to be the going rate at the time. I thought to myself that maybe I should have tried my luck down south earlier, when I had the chance of a trial with Bolton.

I came home from the pit one afternoon and met Irwin. We chatted for a wee while and then I signed for the Quakers on 21 April 1951. I didn't receive any signing-on fee. So off I went down to England, but I just didn't like it very much and became homesick, missing Loanhead and my family.

I scored on my home debut on 22 August 1951 in our 2–1 win over Rochdale, although it must be said that my entry into the English League was far from auspicious. I just could not settle at Feethams and in February 1952 I asked for my release after my final appearance, a 1–0 victory over York City on 9 February 1952 – I finished with them soon after. They did have some good players, like right-back Joe Davison, who left soon after me and who made 240 League appearances, scoring seven goals, and Harry Yates, who made over 100 senior appearances.

It was while I was with Darlington that I became good friends with the Italian-born goalkeeper Rolando Ugolini. When I was with Oldham, I met up with him again socially. Roly, as he was known, was at Middlesbrough and I often went to watch him play. He came to Scotland at the age of three and his parents had a fish and chip shop in Armadale. He was a very agile and acrobatic goalkeeper with his hair slicked back and his sleeves rolled up and his nickname was 'the Cat'. He started with Celtic in 1944 but played just five senior games. He played over 300 League games for 'Boro before he moved to Wrexham in 1957. He ended his career with Berwick Rangers in 1962, and after retiring he became a bookie.

On to Oldham Athletic

After leaving Darlington I went back home and returned to the pit for a few weeks again as a labourer. One Sunday I received three telegrams: from Dundee United, Arbroath and Oldham Athletic. How they learnt about me, I'm not quite sure.

As the money was better in England, I rang up the Oldham player-manager George Hardwick on the Monday morning. He said that he would like to have me on board and that I should come down. I went, they found me lodgings, we talked a wee while and I signed with them in February 1952. I was on wages of £14 per week plus bonuses of £2 for a win and £1 for a draw. I had to pay £1 for the lodgings, which I really hated staying in.

Hardwick had a long-playing career with both Middlesborough and Oldham with a total of 333 appearances and 19 goals. He also won 13 caps for England and later went on to manage PSV Eindhoven, Sunderland and the Dutch national side.

I scored for Oldham on my home debut on 8 March 1952, a 1–0 victory over Stockport County, but in truth I just wasn't happy with the set-up at Boundary Park.

There was a lot of infighting, and it just wasn't a happy club at all with too many chiefs. They kept telling me what style to play and I told them, 'You can't tell anybody how to play'. I wanted to play as an attacking centre-forward and so they hardly picked me. I played just five League games and then I asked for a transfer.

While at Oldham I met up with an old friend, Peter McKennan. The 34-year-old veteran was coming to the end of his career with the Latics. Throughout his career he was known as 'Ma Ba' (my ball); he derived his nickname from his habit of always screaming in his Scottish accent for the ball, no matter what position he was in on the field. We weren't real buddy buddies, but Peter would borrow George Hardwick's car and we would travel to Manchester to do some shopping. We also socialised with the other Oldham players, going to club social dances and the like. It was while I was at Oldham that I first met my future wife Jean.

Time to move on again... signed by Norwich City
Oldham informed me that I would receive a free transfer at the end of the season, but unbeknown to me, both Tommy Bradshaw (the

Peter Stuart McKennan was born in Airdrie on 16 July 1918. The forward became one of the great celebrities of the thirties and forties in the Scottish game with Partick Thistle, for whom he made over 200 appearances, scoring over 100 goals. He came south of the border to play for Chelsea during World War Two and in October 1947 he joined West Bromwich Albion. He then played with Leicester City, Brentford, Middlesbrough and finally Oldham before joining Coleraine in Northern Ireland in 1954 as player-coach. He retired from the game in 1956. He made a total of 101 League appearances, scoring 63 goals. McKennan died in Dundonald on 28 September 1991, aged 73.

chief scout), and Norman Low (the manager of Norwich City), were at the Oldham versus Mansfield Town match in May 1952. It was the final League match of the season, and it attracted 5,593 fans. Tommy and Norman came to watch me play, liked what they saw and asked permission from the Oldham directors to talk to me. We beat Mansfield 5–3 and, right on cue, I netted two goals.

When I went down to sign for Norwich City I met their manager Norman Low and he asked me what I thought about the club and its ground. I said, 'Yeah, it's a good'un.' Low told me he was very pleased with the way I played. He thought I had a nice direct style. Norwich offered Oldham £500 for me, which was accepted by the Oldham board, who kept quiet about the fact that I was available on a free transfer.

I told Low and Bradshaw that if they let me play my direct way, I would score goals for them. For a while Low did just that and let me get on with it. I got the same money as with Oldham, £14. When I

Newcastle-born Norman Low had experience as a player with Liverpool in the 1930s and Newport County in 1946. He also made 163 senior appearances for the Canaries in 1946–50, many as captain, before being appointed manager. He managed Norwich for 258 games and was their third most successful manager. He later managed both Workington and then Port Vale, who were Fourth Division champions under his leadership in 1958.

went back to Oldham after signing the forms for Norwich I asked Jean to marry me and we were married on 19 July 1952. We moved to Norwich and shared a club house with the City goalkeeper, Manchester-born Ken Oxford, and his wife Joan. I was sorry to hear of Ken Oxford's death in August 1993 after a long career with City and Derby County that extended to 299 career League appearances. Ken Oxford will be remembered by older Orient supporters for one of the finest goalkeeping displays ever seen at Brisbane Road for Norwich City in 9 April 1955.

I scored a goal on my Canaries debut on 23 August 1952 against Aldershot and we won 5–0 in front of a wonderful crowd of 27,243 spectators. I soon found my feet at Carrow Road, becoming an instant hit with 10 goals from the first 10 games. This included four goals in my seventh match, which was an 8–1 victory over Shrewsbury Town at Gay Meadow.

I really enjoyed the Norwich City style of play, and in fact the general standard in the Third Division South was better than my experience of the Third Division North. I also liked playing in front of some large crowds, which helped my game.

Soon after I joined Norwich, Tom Bradshaw told me that one of his best mates, Matt Busby from Manchester United, was also at the Oldham game I had played in when they had come to watch me. Busby had told Bradshaw that he was watching the big blonde craggy Scot with a view of putting an offer in, but when he was told about the Norwich bid (with Bradshaw being a mate of his), Busby told him to go ahead and make his offer. He said that he would back away, and so as not to lose face he intimated that he was really looking for someone much younger to join his 'Busby Babes' squad. I was one month off my 25th birthday at the time.

During late 1954, Manchester United came to Carrow Road to play a hospital charity match. After the game Matt Busby came up to me and paid me a great compliment. He said: 'You have done something today that I've not seen anyone else do in all my time at Old Trafford' and I said 'What was that?'. He replied: 'Tommy, well you were just brilliant, the way you won every ball in the air against our great centre-half Allenby Chilton'. I joked with him: 'At least I'm doing something right'. Busby considered Chilton the best centre-half of his long reign at Old Trafford.

I'm not sure if it meant anything, maybe it was just a so-called coincidence, but Chilton was sold a few months later to Grimsby Town after more than 350 League appearances for United. I put one over Chilton again three years later when he was manager at Grimsby Town, netting three against his side for Orient. I also did well against them when I was with Blackburn, scoring twice in a 3–0 win on my Rovers debut in March 1958.

Allenby Chilton was born in South Hylton, County Durham, on 16 September 1918. Before taking up football he trained to become a professional boxer. He started his football career with Seaham Harbour and he joined Manchester United in November 1938 after being on the books of Liverpool as an amateur. He was a United regular for nine seasons, winning an FA Cup-winners' medal in 1948 and a League Championship medal in 1952. He totalled 432 senior appearances for United, scoring three goals between 1939–55. He was considered by many to be one of the most powerful stoppers of his era. He won two England caps and was in the 1954 England World Cup squad. He became player-manager of Grimsby Town in March 1955 and later had a short time as boss of Wigan Athletic in May 1960. He managed Hartlepool United for the 1962–63 season. He died in Southwick on 15 June 1996, aged 78.

I imagined myself signing for Manchester United – me, an ex-coal miner from a Loanhead pit. I thought of all the great players they'd got – I'd have had to have played well every week just to keep a place in the reserves. All those top names: Duncan Edwards, Bobby Charlton, Dennis Violet. I thought that it wasn't for me.

A year later Fulham came to Norwich to play in the same hospital charity competition and they had a former Manchester United player in their side named Charlie Mitten. I remember Charlie was a good player, and also in their side was a young lad named Johnny Haynes who played inside-left. He started to swear on the pitch and it was all directed at Mitten. I said to Charlie, 'I wouldn't take that from that young little bugger'. He replied 'What can I do, he's a great 'un, you can't say anything to him', and he ran off. He was right – Haynes was a grand player and a loyal Fulham man. He stayed at Craven Cottage throughout his 17 years in football, making 594 League appearances and scoring 145 goals. He also won 56 caps for England.

Two goals knock Arsenal out of the FA Cup at Highbury

I remember with fondness the Canaries' great FA Cup victory over Arsenal at Highbury. The Gunners were League champions at the time. I only played at the last minute because Johnny Summers failed a late fitness test.

I was pleased as punch that I was playing, and I headed two goals to knock the mighty Arsenal out of the FA Cup in a 2–1 win. The home team had been leading 1–0 through a Jimmy Logie penalty, and all the drama was played out before the largest crowd I had ever seen, of 55,767. My first header was from a Johnny Gavin cross and the second, 20 minutes later, came from a Peter Gordon cross.

My Dad was a very proud man that day back home in Loanhead. The local newspaper carried the story of his son, Thomas Johnston and the great hero he had become in Norwich. Dad had become a great hero himself in Loanhead because of my achievements. The Norwich boss Norman Low told the press: 'Tom is our best bargain, he's just brilliant when the ball is in the air.'

When we got back to Norwich from Highbury all the players were invited back to the Blue Room, which was a pub just on the bridge in the city. When we got off the train we were mobbed by the home fans. Dennis Morgan and myself jumped over the railway line so we could be first in the pub. The barmaid said 'Oh, you are our Norwich players', and we said we were. She said that her boss had said that anything we drank was on him.

We had quite a few drinks during the evening. A supporter came over, he also looked a bit the worse for wear. He said 'Well played my boys, I can't buy you a drink but you can have these' and he gave us a bundle of sausages. So when I left the pub and eventually got home at about 1am it was with a load of sausages in my pocket from this bloke.

The next day, after sobering up, all the players went to meet the Mayor of Norwich, Mr R.H. Mottram, who gave a speech and also made me a special toast congratulating me on my achievements at Highbury. These were happy times.

However, any hopes of a Cup Final medal were dashed when we were knocked out of the FA Cup in the fifth round at home. We lost to Leicester City 2–1 in front of nearly 40,000 fans.

I was playing well for Norwich City and became their star player after the Highbury match, but I then got injured. I pulled a muscle and I was advised by the club doctor to rest the injury for several months, but the boss wanted me playing. The coach got me running up and down the terracing steps, which caused me even more pain and problems.

Nevertheless I continued playing and scored just six goals from the following 15 appearances, two of the goals coming in an exciting 4–4 draw at Reading and two in a 3–1 win over Leyton Orient.

There was a lot of competition for the number nine jersey from centre-forwards like Roy Hollis and Johnny Summers, who were both with the Canaries at the time.

In any fictional story, my great day at Highbury would have been the turning point of my career, leading on to fame and fortune – but this was real life and not the stage or some novelist's manuscript. I had a few years to wait before I became a nationally recognised player down in East London with the Orient.

I made a lot of good friends at Norwich: right-back Dennis Morgan, who made 250 senior appearances for the Canaries; their brave goalie Ken Nethercott, who spent 12 loyal years at Carrow Road making 416 senior appearances; also Bobby Brennan (220 appearances); and John Duffy (78 League appearances). There were also my very good friends Noel Kinsey and Johnny Summers.

Things began to change after a while at Carrow Road and not for the better. The directors decided in their wisdom that they wanted to run the show. They were telling manager Low who should be in the team and how they should play. One of the ideas at the time was playing the Revie plan, with a deep-lying centre-forward to draw defenders out of position, so creating space for the inside-forwards in the penalty area.

Just a short time after this, the famous Sunderland player Len Shackleton wrote a book and on one page of his book he wrote: 'Directors' knowledge of football' and left the rest of the page blank. How right he was. As things got worse at Norwich City I decided I wanted away from Carrow Road.

The Don Revie Plan

In September 1954, the Norwich directors wanted to me to change my style of play to fit in with the latest fashion in football – the 'Revie and McDowell' plan. This was brought into the game during the 1954–55 season by the Manchester City manager Leslie McDowell and centre-forward Don Revie. A blackboard was used to show the players how to move. They would tell you that when your marker was standing there, you would move here, and so on and so on. I found this virtually impossible – I couldn't see how I could wait to see whether player 'A' would move to position 'B'.

I thought to myself that if all of the teams played the Revie plan, centre-forwards like me would be out of favour and even out of a job. The plan for a deep-lying centre-forward was first introduced by Hungary when they thrashed England 6–3 at Wembley in November 1953.

It was their centre-forward Nandor Hidegkuti (see p162 Chapter 12, 'What the Press Said', on Johnston being compared with the Hungarian player) who dropped back into a deeper role, which greatly confused the England defenders. This allowed the Hungarians' two inside-forwards, Sandor Koscis and Ferenc Puskas, much more space down the middle of the park with the English defenders being pulled out of position. Manchester City was the first club to hit on the idea and try to adopt the new style of play.

McDowell had the City players back early for training during June 1954 to copy the Hungarian style with Revie playing in this deeper role. The emphasis was on the passing game rather than individual skills and it certainly worked for a while.

Revie was voted player of the year and Manchester City reached the final of the FA Cup at Wembley twice in two years. The first time they lost, but in the second final in May 1956 they beat Birmingham City 3–1. As teams changed their tactics to counteract the Revie plan, things began to fall apart and City were relegated twice during the late fifties.

A large number of managers within the higher divisions started to follow City and the Continentals, implementing the Hungarian or Revie style of play – whatever they called it. This happened even to the extent of players wearing tighter and shorter-looking shorts! I told manager Norman Low that I was sticking rigidly to my long shorts – I told him: 'A pair of shorts don't make the player.' Thankfully, these fads didn't last too long.

I was in the team for one match, then in the reserves the next so I went to see manager Low about being dropped and he said: 'I would have you in my side every week, but it is the directors who pick the team'. I said to him 'In that case, why are you employed at the club if the directors are picking your team?' I suppose to be fair to Low this was happening quite a bit at a number of clubs during that era.

Anyway, I ignored the new Revie style and I played with the flow of the game and yes, 'I did it my way', but Low didn't like it – so after various confrontations with him I fell out of favour. Both Bristol Rovers and Watford had made enquiries about me and they were told that I would be playing for the Norwich reserve side at St Andrews. When we arrived the reserve trainer Harry Proctor told me I wasn't playing and I asked why. He replied: 'I've just been told at the hotel by the directors that Johnston must not play, another player must play at centre-forward instead'.

When I got back to Carrow Road, I was told that the directors had said 'If you are selling a racehorse, you don't run it'. Their mentality left me speechless. Len Shackleton was quite right, the directors' knowledge of football was non-existent. It was just stupid in my book, but I suppose they had the money to put into the club and they felt that bought them the right to make decisions. Anyway, I became very unhappy about the situation and wanted to leave East Anglia. I was no failure with the Canaries, bagging 33 goals from 67 senior appearances – and of course I had had that wonderful day at Highbury.

One of the hardest and best centre-halves I ever played against was while I was with the Canaries and that was Newport County's Ray Wilcox. I never ever got any change out of him, and in fact he was known as a hard man. When I joined the Welsh side myself, I soon realised that he was a real gentleman off the field. Ray played over 500 senior games for County and, after retiring in 1959, he became their trainer. Sadly, he died in Newport on 26 January 2003, aged 81. He had a brother, Caradoc, who also played at Newport.

Newport, here I come

An offer came in for me from Newport County and on 16 October 1954 I signed for them for a fee of £2,100. Their player-manager was Billy Lucas and he was a man of vision. The Revie plan was not used as much, and he said: 'Get down the middle, the old fashioned way, and we will get the ball over to you'. They did, and it worked. My weekly wage remained at £14.

> *William Henry Lucas was born in Newport in 1918 and won eight full and seven wartime caps for Wales. He made 445 League career appearances, scoring 72 goals, and he died during 1998, having suffered from Alzheimer's disease for many years.*

I scored twice at Torquay United soon after signing for County and I was a much happier man. This showed in my performances, as I scored goal after goal and did not look back. I took the odd penalty for County and did alright – my philosophy was to hit them hard so that if the goalie touched it, they wouldn't be able to stop it. I cracked one past the Leyton Orient goalkeeper Pat Welton in April 1955.

I remember one match, a benefit game on 5 May 1955. It was an unbelievable game with Stanley Matthews, Tom Finney, Harry Johnston, Jimmy Hagan, Trevor Ford, Mel Charles, Derek Tapscott, Ivor Allchurch and Peter Doherty playing for the opposition, and Newport were losing 8–7 with just minutes to go. We got a penalty in the dying seconds and the 15,636 spectators went wild at the prospect of drawing against these great stars.

I stepped up. I thought 'I must score with this kick, we can't get beat 8–7'. The fans stood right round from the left corner flag, across the back of the goal to the right corner flag. If I had missed the kick, I would have hit a number of them in the face or something. Anyway, I hit the ball straight and hard and I scored. For me it was a personal triumph. I had bagged six goals, with Les Graham and Harry Harris scoring the other two goals. The goalscorers for the All Stars XI were: Allchurch, three; Ford, three; and Tapscott and Charles, one each.

After the match, the crowd invaded the pitch and the police had to escort Stanley Matthews across the field and out of the ground. A taxi was waiting to speed him away to the station, as he would never have got out of the ground. He played very well that night, and he was a very popular man. I felt privileged to have been on the same pitch as these stars, they were great players and I learnt a lot from them.

As our player-manager stated: 'There can be no grumbles about the entertainment, with 16 goals in the match.'

I heard that Stanley Matthews got £100 to appear in benefit games. It was worth giving him that sort of money to play because he drew the large crowds. Newport had not seen a crowd of over 15,000 in years.

I enjoyed my stay with Newport County, making 68 League and FA Cup appearances and scoring 53 goals. Even though they were near the bottom of the Third Division South and the club was short of cash, they were playing pretty well and I never had any problems. Everything was going well for me personally, so I didn't really want to leave Wales. After all, I never missed a single senior match for them. I also played in three Welsh Cup matches and scored six goals, including a hat-trick against Barry Town during January 1956 in a game we won 8–1.

Anthony Ambrosen, the historian of Newport County, said:

Tommy Johnston was one of our star players. The season after he left for Leyton Orient, we were right up there pushing for promotion to Division Two with Pat Terry and former Orient man Mike Burgess leading the front line. In all honesty, they were not Johnston and if the craggy Scot had stayed with us, there was no doubt he would have scored a lot of goals and I'm sure we would have had a great chance of promotion, but instead our run just fizzled out.

Chapter 4

Happy times with Leyton Orient

I heard that Leyton Orient wanted me to join them. Funnily enough I had played against them twice that season and scored four goals in those matches. I enjoyed playing against Stan Aldous, and in fact I had played against him five times in my career – with Orient, Norwich and Newport – and scored eight goals. One was a penalty.

After I had joined them, one day in the dressing room Aldous told me the story of how and why the offer for me was made.

During January 1956, when Orient were travelling home on the train from an away League match at Coventry City, which they had lost 3–0, chairman Harry Zussman was discussing with the players the need for a quality centre-forward to strengthen the push for the Third Division championship. He said: 'We must have one, any suggestions?'

Aldous, the captain of the side shouted out, 'Yes, I reckon we ought to go for that fellow Johnston from Newport County. He always plays a blinder against me, in fact he is an absolute menace'. O's caretaker manager Les Gore then had a quiet chat with two Orient players with Welsh backgrounds, asking them if they would be interested in moving to Newport as part of a transfer deal, but both players were married and had just bought homes in London, so they turned the idea down.

Signing for Orient at Newport Station

A week or so later I appeared for Newport at Brisbane Road and scored with a bullet trademark header. Orient were impressed and the offer was put in for me. I got wind of a possible deal when the O's player Stan Charlton came up to me after that match and said, 'how do you fancy playing for Leyton Orient?' and I replied 'I'll play for anyone if they pay me'.

The Newport manager Billy Lucas had asked me to accompany him to London to meet with Mike Burgess, Orient's Canadian-born number nine, who had been asked about whether he would be interested in a move to Newport as part of my transfer deal. On arrival at Paddington Station we had lunch in the hotel and it was my job to persuade Burgess of the benefits of joining Newport County. It worked and he agreed terms. Lucas and I caught the afternoon train back to Newport. In 2004 Mike said:

> Yes, Orient officials did approach me about a move to Newport County and we arranged a meeting at Paddington Railway Station Hotel. Billy Lucas, the Newport manager, and Tommy Johnston were at the meeting where a deal was struck concerning financial terms for both Johnston and myself. On reflection about the move to Newport, I was never really happy there. However, it was a stepping stone for me and I was transferred to Bournemouth and spent four happy years with them.

Burgess went on to make a career total of 314 League appearances with 58 goals.

The arrangement was that O's secretary Arthur Huggett would return to Newport with my contract on the following Friday morning, which he did. I signed it and he returned immediately to London to deposit the contract with the Football League in London so I would be able to play the next day at Swindon. That evening, I was contacted by the club to say that everything was in order.

I was told to get to Swindon Town's ground by 2pm, which I did. I was only officially introduced to the Orient players on the field.

Newport had been short of cash, which was why they had agreed to sell me. It was Les Gore who actually signed me for Leyton Orient (not, as many thought, Alex Stock) for £5,500. Mike Burgess was valued at £2,000. No one was more surprised and thrilled by the news of my signing than Stan Aldous and Stan Charlton. It was only later that I was informed that the £5,500 for the deal was paid out of Harry Zussman's own pocket.

The Newport supporters were shell-shocked by the news of my departure – they thought that I was one of their best players and they were worried that the board had sold me for a small profit.

Aldous was a top-notch centre-half, having played (when I joined the O's), 240 senior games for Orient. He went on to record a total of 327 senior games for them, so he clearly knew a bit about the

Research by the authors shows that only four centre-forwards ever managed to score a hat-trick against Stan Aldous in his 327 appearances for the Londoners. He was one of the most respected defenders in the Third Division. Those players were: Albert Campbell 'Cam' Burgess, who scored three for Crystal Palace at Brisbane Road on 15 September 1951 (Palace won 4–0) in Division Three South; John Shepherd, who scored four for Millwall at Leyton on 25 October 1952 (Millwall won 4–1) in Division Three South, this was Shepherd's Football League debut; Jack Hudson for Shrewsbury Town at Shrewsbury on 24 October 1953 (a 3–3 draw); and Tommy Johnston, who scored three for Newport County at Newport on 8 October 1955.

The most notable aspect of Johnston's hat-trick was that it was against an O's side pushing for the championship with the best defensive record in the division. When the other three netted their goals, O's were in a lowly position in the League table.

decent centre-forwards around at the time. In the end, it was me he recommended. I had most certainly been Stan Aldous's bogey player and I know he was very happy that we were now on the same side.

So now I was a Leyton Orient player. Les Gore allowed me to play the way I wanted to play as he wasn't really in favour of the Revie plan, although in later seasons, like most managers, he tried it out. I was on wages of £14 per week (which rose, at last, to £20 after we entered the Second Division – the wage-capping amount had increased).

A row, then meeting with Alec Stock

However, things soon changed at the club. Alec Stock returned from Arsenal in April 1956. He had been the Gunners' assistant manager, but he was away for just 53 days from Leyton Orient. When he returned he said in the club programme that he had missed the Orient too much. He wanted to introduce the Revie plan, which was obviously used at Highbury, in Orient's final promotion push. He started telling me how to play, saying 'play deeper, play deeper'. He wanted me to take the centre-half out of the middle and allow the inside-forwards in. I was not happy about that and I told him so. He was not at all thrilled with me.

Stock called me into his office and insisted that I play his way. I said: 'Many have tried this plan but it didn't work. I want to play my old way but if you want me to play your way, you go up in front of the supporters on the loud speaker'. (They were getting an average of 16,000 people for each home match.) 'Tell them that Tommy Johnston is playing your "new way" and that I'm not scoring any goals. It will be your fault that we don't win promotion.'

Stock said, 'I will not do that', and then he threatened me, saying he could get someone else in to take my place who would play his style. I replied: 'Well, you just get them in and you find me another club'.

I went to see Harry Zussman, the chairman about the matter afterwards, and as far as I was concerned that was the end of it. I was never dropped by Stock, and he never mentioned it to me again. He didn't find me another club either, so Zussman must have done his job. It would have been hard for them to sell me when I was rattling the net so regularly.

It wasn't really a falling out that I had with Stock, it was just that he wanted me to play his way and I wanted to do it my way. I suppose I was being a stubborn Scot and he was a stubborn Englishman! I knew if I played his way that the goals would dry up and the fans would be unhappy with him, the team and me, and we could miss out on winning the championship. Anyway, it all turned out well in the end and Les Gore understood my reaction. He calmed me down, but I never forgot the confrontation with Mr Stock.

My first medal in football as Orient win promotion

Towards the end of the 1955–56 season, I found myself in a team fighting a promotion battle and there were plenty of thrills before we beat Millwall 2–1, steering our way into the Second Division. I remember that on Easter Saturday we were at home to Brighton, who were pushing us for the top spot. Only one team was promoted in those days. Two points from this match would have been a 'four pointer', and we felt pretty confident because the team had recorded 10 straight wins on the trot and scored 33 goals. But we came unstuck and they beat us by a single goal in front of over 25,500 fans. I left the field feeling it was my fault. I had missed a sitter, the kind of chance a centre-forward seeks all through a match – right in front of an open goal.

Fortunately for me, the tension was eased on the Easter Monday when we won at Torquay 3–1. Then came the big day: a victory over struggling Millwall at Brisbane Road on 26 April 1956. This assured us of the championship – but what sweat and strain had been endured, not only by the players, but also by the 22,337 fans. As Roy Peskett wrote in the *Daily Mail*: 'The O's fans literally were seen praying for their team'. In the end we came out on top and gained promotion, but believe me it was a tough match.

The first half ended goalless; it seemed inevitable that strange things would happen, and so it proved when Johnny Hartburn swung over a corner kick. I was waiting for it in the middle, thinking it would reach either Phil (Woosnam) or myself, but instead it swung straight into the net, curling inside the near post. That was on 51 minutes, so we were one up. Hartburn told me after the match that it was only the second time in his long career that he had scored in this way.

The Lions were still fighting for their lives and it was my old Norwich City mate Johnny Summers who scored for them after a rare mistake by our defender Jack Gregory. Then, with just 19 minutes remaining, came one of the sweetest moments of my career when a header from our skipper Stan Aldous reached me and I thumped it into the roof of the net. After a further 20 minutes or so, the referee Mervyn Griffiths blew the final whistle and victory was ours by 2–1 – so Orient made it, reaching the Second Division for the first time since 1929.

The fans went crazy with delight and so did I. After all it was my first taste of success, winning a Championship medal. Then came the speeches and the champagne flowed. It crowned a wonderful season for the club, its Chairman Harry Zussman, Les Gore and Alec Stock and all the players and supporters.

The final three matches of the season were a bit of an anticlimax. We lost all of them, one being a 5–0 defeat at Millwall. I remember after all the celebrations the whole squad returned to the ground and, in one rare moment of quiet, we had a photo taken with the Championship shield. It was nice for all the players to have time together to reflect on our success, after all it was the first time Leyton Orient had won anything in the Football League since joining it in the 1905–06 season.

Division Three South 1955–56 – (only one team promoted) – Final top three places

	P	W	D	L	F	A	Pts
Leyton Orient	46	29	8	9	106	49	66
Brighton & Hove Albion	46	29	7	10	112	50	65
Ipswich Town	46	25	14	7	106	60	64

In August 1957 Alec Stock surprisingly left the club for the second time as we were about to start our Second Division campaign. He went to manage Roma in Italy, and I for one was happy that Les Gore was back as manager.

Our campaign in the Second Division started off in poor fashion with a 4–1 home defeat by Nottingham Forest. It was my mate, Dave Sexton, who scored our goal on his debut before over 25,000 fans.

I only got onto the scoresheet in our fifth match, scoring the winner in a 4–3 win over Bury. On 15 September 1957 we were playing Doncaster Rovers and my marker was Charlie Williams and I was continually being intimidated and fouled. After a free-kick came into the box, I was elbowed in the face by him. Me and most of the nearly-20,000 crowd were amazed when the referee sent *me* off. The club decided to appeal against the referee's decision.

It appears that a letter was sent to the Football Association from a neutral observer at the match, which explained in detail what he witnessed. After viewing all the evidence, the FA disciplinary committee took the unusual step of not taking any further action against me.

I must say that I had played against Williams on a number of occasions and he was never a dirty player. Hard, yes, but never dirty, so one can only assume that he must having been playing under instructions from the Doncaster manager, an old friend of mine, Peter Doherty.

After our poor start to the season we managed to recover to a respectable 15th position and I bagged a healthy 27 League goals.

The following season also started off badly for us. We had a very

Charlie Williams was born in Royston, near Barnsley, on 23 December 1928 – his father originally came from Barbados. He left school at 14 to go down the mines and went on to spend 12 years playing for Doncaster Rovers, making 157 League appearances, scoring once. He eventually became a comedian and broke through on Granada Television show The Comedians *in the 1960s and was the first black comedian to appear on British mainstream television – and a great success he was too.*

heavy 7–2 defeat at Grimsby Town, although I netted both our goals. Two further defeats soon followed, but then things began to pick up a little and I scored 11 goals in eight matches, although we achieved just three wins.

We often went on training camps down at the coast to get away from things, usually to Ramsgate, which was a favourite place to prepare for important League games. All this was paid for by Messrs Grade, Young and Zussman.

I could see Les Gore was getting a little worried about the lack of success, and in one match against Middlesbrough on 28 September 1957 he said to me, 'what do you think about playing a little deeper?' He asked me if I would drop further back, the Revie way, and play at inside-left to take the defenders away from the goalmouth, hoping that we could surprise them and Len Julians could find extra space in the box to score. I wasn't happy about it, but for Les I agreed to try it.

I just wasn't getting into the flow of the game, it really wasn't my style to play in this way and the plan wasn't working, so we decided that I should move further up field again to take on the centre-half and it worked. I still became the goal provider. Julians got in the game much more, and he was finding a lot of space, so much so that he scored all our four goals. We only played this Revie way for a few more games and it was dropped after we suffered a 3–1 defeat at Fulham. Les Gore decided to revert to our normal style and we then thrashed Swansea Town 5–1 on 26 October 1957. I bagged a hat-trick – so much for the Revie plan! It just didn't work for a player like me.

When I hit my third goal, which I slid under the body of the advancing Swansea Town goalie Robert Reid, his leg got caught up with mine and I went tumbling down over him. I thought I had injured him and was more worried about picking him up and ensuring he was alright than celebrating my hat-trick. I only realised the ball was in the back of the net when Eddie Brown patted me on the back in congratulations and I heard the roar of the Leyton fans in celebration.

I think at the time we had one of the best forward lines in the Second Division with players like White, Woosnam, Johnston, Julians and Heckman.

Over the next few months, everything went very well for me with the Orient. I was becoming the talk of the football world with my scoring feats, and I scored 19 League and FA Cup goals in just 10 matches between the end of November 1957 and January 1958.

After the 12 goals I scored in December 1957, a national newspaper visited Jean and me at our Essex home to meet the family and take some photos for an article on me. The pictures came out very well.

Jinx man, Tommy Younger

Les Gore asked me to take the team's penalties, and I knocked in a couple, but then I came up against my 'jinx man', Liverpool's Tommy Younger. I thought my old mining mate would know exactly where I was going to put my spot kick. I went up and tried to confuse him and change the direction and kicked it the other way. I mis-kicked the ball and he just walked across his goal, saved my kick and said 'thank you very much Mr Johnston'. In the end, the only thing I did was to confuse myself. I got one against Barnsley in October, but missed another the following month against Notts County, so missing out on another hat-trick.

'Never again', I said to the boss, so I gave that away and stopped taking them.

We blended well as a team and we were very strong on the right flank but I had to convince young Phil Woosnam on a number of different occasions that we were in fact playing on the same side. Phil tended to hang onto the ball too long, which upset the front line. I eventually spoke to him and asked him what colour jersey I was wearing. When he replied 'royal blue,' I said 'yes, the same as you Phil'. After that, it was only a matter of saying 'now Phil' and the ball was there. Phil turned out to be the best player I played with in my long career, and he deserved the international recognition that he attained with Wales.

One of the real characters at the club was wing man Mark Lazarus. His family followed and supported him at both home and away games where his clan acted as his cheerleaders. I could quote many priceless comments made by Mark. He once told me in all seriousness at training that his brother was getting out on Friday. I said 'Is he in the Army?' and his reply was 'No, in jail'. I think this may have been his Cockney wit!

The club was converting a house into two flats to be used by Ron Foster and Mark, and the flats were being redecorated. Mark and his wife went to view the finished job and his comment was: 'Aren't these fellows clever, they know exactly where to cut the doors and windows out!' The rest of his comments aren't really suitable for publication.

If Stock returns, I leave

I was happy at Leyton Orient and had no thoughts of leaving. The directors and Les Gore were happy with me too, and Les was still caretaker manager. However, I heard that Alec Stock was coming back again to be the manager and I had a meeting with Gore. I told him that if Stock did come back to Leyton at the end of February 1958, I was for the off. Les always knew how I felt about playing Stock's way, and we were good friends.

I had also confided in chief scout Sid Hobbins about my feelings regarding Stock's return to the club. Sid felt the same way and didn't want Stock back either. He felt that Stock was just using the club – always leaving for so-called better jobs, yet always returning to get his job back when things weren't working out for him elsewhere.

Harry Zussman asked me to come to his shoe factory in Shoreditch. Les Gore was there too and they offered me a deal to stay with the club. It was a job for life with Leyton Orient. I thought to myself about what it would be like to play for Alec Stock again and decided I didn't want to play under his leadership.

That was one of the reasons why I decided to leave the Orient and join Blackburn Rovers. The talk of a Scottish cap and the lure of playing First Division football did play a big part in it too – after all it was my last chance to play in the higher grade, and I was not going to achieve this with the Orient. But it was the return to the club of Mr Stock from Italy that really forced me to make up my mind to leave Brisbane Road. He was away for just three months in Italy.

It was during this time that Hobbins and club secretary Huggett were both asked to leave the club over some internal irregularities. The players didn't really know what that was all about. Anyway we knew both men were very upset and, to get back in some way at the club, Hobbins phoned all the leading newspapers and told them about the comments I had made to him in confidence concerning Stock. The story never really hurt the club but it did make me look like the bad guy.

Daily Express article causes a big rumpus

After the departure of Hobbins and Huggett, but before my move to Blackburn, I thought it very strange that suddenly all the newspapers wanted to interview me for what I was told was a story about my goalscoring achievements. Les Gore gave me permission to be interviewed by Roger Malone of the *Daily Express*, who came to the house to see me. The interview turned into a real debacle.

All hell broke loose when the *Express* story hit the streets. Les Gore and Alec Stock (in Italy) were furious and I wasn't very happy either with the trick the *Express* reporter pulled. The whole story was about my thoughts on Alec Stock and not about my goalscoring feats. That newspaper was in the club's bad books for a long time after that.

I explained to Gore that the story was twisted all out of context. It was revealed some months later that the problem the club had with both Hobbins and Huggett was down to a so-called misunderstanding. I'm not sure what happened after that, but Hobbins died in Woolwich, London on 16 March 1984. I did receive a letter from his sons during the 1957–58 season saying how they followed my career with great interest and how they kept all the articles on me (they were probably totally unaware of the happenings of the past).

Although I had made those comments about Stock, I had spoken to both Les Gore and Hobbins in confidence, and it was never meant for public consumption. I definitely did not intend for my words to be splashed over the sports pages of a national newspaper.

I would much rather have stayed with Leyton Orient and played out my career with them. I'm sure old Dixie Dean's record would have been in reach that season, but the deal went through and I was off to Blackburn for £15,000, teaming up with Johnny Carey and playing alongside some big-name players.

This wasn't the first time that the Rovers boss Johnny Carey had tried to sign me. When Orient had thrashed Rovers 5–1 on 7 December 1957 and I had scored twice, Carey and the Rovers vice-chairman Mr J. Wilkinson were so impressed with my performance that they put in a £10,000 bid for me. For over an hour they tried to persuade the Orient board to part with me, but I heard they got a blank refusal. Carey had come back two weeks later but Harry Zussman had refused the terms. Then, once I heard that Alec Stock was coming back and I put in my transfer request, the club notified Johnny Carey to tell him I was available.

I put pen to paper just 3½ hours before Rovers were due to play Grimsby Town. I was told that Carey had sought some of the top centre-forwards around like Don Kichenbrand from Glasgow Rangers, Gerry Hitchens of Cardiff City, Alf Ackerman of Carlisle United and Ken Johnson of Hartlepools United – but it was me he really wanted.

Johnny Carey told a local Blackburn newspaper:

> After we were unable to sign the Bolton centre-forward Nat Lofthouse, I put in several offers for Tommy Johnston and after three months I eventually got him. I am sure he is the player to help take us up to the First Division. He has been the man I most wanted to replace Tommy Briggs who had lost form.

Signing for Blackburn Rovers, winning a second medal

Johnny Carey told me that he was one of the managers who had previously used the Revie plan but he had decided that it was time to revert to the old way. He said he had searched all over the country and that I was one of the best old-fashioned centre-forwards around, able to score the goals and allow space for the other forwards. This was what he thought was needed to get Rovers promoted.

I signed for Rovers on 7 March 1958. At the time they were not a certainty to go up to the First Division, but I thought to myself that with me in the side, they might just make it. My wife, on the other hand, was not at all keen on the move northwards – she was settled and loved living in Essex.

Johnny Carey was a well-respected man in football after his great playing career with Manchester United – and Blackburn was, I suppose, an alright club. They had some very good players in their ranks like Bryan Douglas, Roy Vernon, Peter Dobing and Bill Eckersley. At 30 and 32 years old respectively, me and Bill were the two oldest players on their books. Bill was a great defender and a grand servant to Rovers, making over 400 League appearances during his 13-year stay at Ewood Park.

Like the Orient, Rovers were in the Second Division, but the difference was that they were lying fourth in the table, unlike the O's who could never make it to the top, even though they had some fine players. (I had played against Rovers in December when Orient thrashed them 5–1, and I scored two goals, so they knew all about me and what I could do.)

Carey wanted me to score and also create goals for Roy Vernon, Peter Dobing, Bryan Douglas and Ally McLeod. It worked very well because I was allowed to do it my way. Before I had joined them, Rovers had hit 49 goals in 31 games, but when I joined I gave them a different dimension to their play. I played in the final 11 games and we netted 44 goals. It was all down to Carey's vision – getting me in there to create and score. That was the reason we got promoted.

Carey understood that by keeping me up front as an attacking centre-forward, I was able to score vital goals as well as creating space for others. During those 11 games I scored eight goals myself and created most of the others, and we scored, on average, four goals per game.

We only lost one match (4–3 at Cardiff City), and had one draw (1–1 at Fulham), from those final 11 games. We won all the rest. We were fighting to gain promotion to get into the First Division and battling against London sides: West Ham United, Charlton Athletic and Fulham, with Liverpool also in contention. Our final game was away at Charlton's Valley ground, where a victory would have assured us of promotion. But if they won, they would take the prize. There were over 56,000 spectators at the Valley and it made for an exciting match. It was a great game and very tense for all concerned.

Unbeknown to anyone at the ground, when I had appeared for Blackburn against the Orient at Ewood Park on 19 April 1957, although we won 4–1, Sid Bishop, the O's top-notch centre-half, had jumped on my little toe during the game and broken it. Despite the injury I was still able to create three goals for Roy Vernon and one for Ally McLeod. In contrast it was probably Sid's worst-ever game for the Orient – serves him right for breaking my toe!

So I played at both Fulham and the Valley with my toes strapped. I couldn't run freely at Craven Cottage, but Johnny Carey wanted me in for the Charlton match because he said 'there would be more confidence in the side' with me there.

I did play, but in a bit of a deeper role as an inside-forward, with Peter Dobing swapping with me and playing at centre-forward. I asked Carey and Dobing if we could change it around if things were not working out, and Carey replied: 'You change it when you want'.

After the first 20 minutes we were a goal down and not creating many chances, so we swapped it around. It certainly worked. I was pulling the Charlton centre-half Derek Ufton out of position, leaving holes up the middle for the others, and we went into the dressing room 3–1 up at half-time.

After half-time Charlton's South African born full-back John Hewie – who actually played for Scotland – scored direct from a free-kick. Then we got a penalty when Ufton pulled me back by the arm as I was about to shoot and Bryan Douglas stepped up to score from the spot. Rovers finished up 4–3 winners. West Ham won 6–1 at Middlesbrough: they ended up as champions and Rovers were also promoted, with both Charlton and Liverpool left in Division Two. It had turned out to be a closely fought battle, as the League table below shows.

Division Two 1957–58 (Top 2 teams promoted) – Final four positions

	P	W	D	L	F	A	Pts
West Ham United	42	23	11	8	101	54	57
Blackburn Rovers	42	22	12	8	93	57	56
Charlton Athletic	42	24	7	11	107	69	55
Liverpool	42	22	11	11	75	50	54

I ended the season as the country's leading marksman with 43 League goals and one FA Cup goal scored for Orient and Blackburn. Although I would soon be 31 years old, I thought to myself that a cap for Scotland could be on the cards, as there were others in the current Scottish squad who were older than me.

The great Brian Clough

During the whole of the 1957–58 season the man who pushed me to become the leading goalscorer in the land was Middlesbrough's Brian Clough. He ended three short of my total at the end of the season on 40 League goals – he was a great goalscorer.

Clough was born in Middlesbrough on 21 March 1935. He was a prolific goalscorer with 'Boro between 1955 and 1960 with 197 goals from 213 League appearances. With Sunderland (1960–64) he netted 54 goals from 61 League appearances. He was the leading marksman in the English League in the 1956–57 season and he finished second behind the leading Division Two marksman for the following six seasons.

He appeared to be a bit of a rebel and an unpopular man with his 'Boro colleagues (not with the fans), and nine fellow 'Boro players signed a petition to the manager to have him removed as the captain. He eventually moved to Sunderland. Injury wrecked his playing career when he was only 29 years old. Like me, he also battled to be recognised at international level when he was scoring regularly with

'Boro, another Second Division side. He won just two caps in 1960 against Wales and Sweden, failing to score in both matches. He went on to become one of the finest managers in football, with both Derby County and Nottingham Forest.

Anyway, I looked at my situation as a First Division player and the leading goalscorer in all four English divisions and I thought 'If this doesn't get me a Scottish cap, then nothing will'.

I was sad to read of the death of Brian Clough, aged 69, on 20 September 2004.

Chapter 5

Dream of playing for Scotland

The dream of any player in whatever sport he or she may be playing in is to represent their country. As the 1957–58 season progressed, I really thought that my time had come and that my long-running dream of playing in the blue of Scotland could become a reality. I knew I had been watched twice by the selectors and I scored six goals in those two matches. I looked at Scotland's recent results and who I would be vying with for the number nine shirt, and I was confident of making it.

In the 1956–57 season Lawrie Reilly was first choice for all of Scotland's matches, but he was now past his best. Reilly was a good centre-forward for Hibernian and also played 38 times for his country, scoring 22 goals. He also netted a total of 234 goals for Hibs, including 18 hat-tricks, and his final appearance for Scotland was early in 1957. Now that Reilly was no longer in contention, the number nine jersey was entrusted to Blackpool's Jackie Mudie.

I did very well in those two League matches when I was watched, as the following press report in the *Daily Express* by the respected sports journalist Bob Pennington proves. I had scored three goals against Grimsby Town on 21 December 1957. Reports in both *The People* and *Daily Express* should have shown my value to the Scottish selectors. Pennington wrote:

> There's no stopping this man Tommy Johnston. The big fair-haired craggy Scot, idol of Brisbane Road fans, added yet another hat-trick to his season goal tally, which now stands at 26, in helping Orient crush Grimsby Town. **The Scots must cap Johnston.**
>
> *The incredible man was just superb. He is the League's leading marksman and looked quite the most dangerous forward I have seen in action this season.* **If the Scots leave him out of their World Cup squad for Sweden, it can only be through sheer prejudice.**

For the second match, against Bristol City, I knew that Matt Busby, the Manchester United manager, had just been appointed as Scotland's part-time boss, and he had asked the selection committee to watch me again. Les Gore told me about this just before kick-off, which inspired me to turn it on against the men from Bristol. Ralph Hadley, in *The People* newspaper of 11 January 1958, wrote:

> This man's a genius – there's no doubt about it. Tommy Johnston of Leyton Orient, I mean. Orient's third goal was the best I've seen. Near the halfway line he beat three Bristol men and swung a long pass into the centre to Phil White, who ran forward to receive it. He had a look round, steadied himself – then across the field he swung a long pass to Johnny Hartburn at outside-left. Who was there to head home the centre? Why Johnston of course. A great goal, a great finish. One of the best I've seen for many a season.

A journalist from the *News of the World* wrote:

> ... the amazing Johnston. Another hat-trick against Bristol City by the brilliant centre-forward brought him to a total of 36 goals this season. He sent the London crowd wild with excitement when he put the seal on a wonderful afternoon's work with a glorious header to complete his

hat-trick eight minutes from the end. Surely, this will impress the Scottish selectors?

The press reports sum it up very well. A number of journalists told me that the selectors had taken back favourable reports on my performances.

I knew for a fact that Matt Busby liked the way I played and that he was looking for something different up front. So, with a few warm-up games to come for the Scots against England, Hungary and Poland, I felt I should be given a chance to prove myself at international level in at least one of those matches – with a good prospect then of making it into their World Cup squad for Sweden.

The Munich air disaster

What no one could know at that time was the terrible event that would shake the football world during the following month. On 6 February 1958, eight Manchester United players died in an air crash near Munich. Manager Matt Busby was one who survived, but he was seriously injured and would only return to office after the World Cup Finals in Sweden. He took charge of two Scottish matches in 1958, when he changed most of the World Cup team; he then decided it was all too much and resigned to concentrate on Manchester United, going back to Old Trafford in July, when he had recovered from his injuries.

At the time of the disaster, I remember receiving an urgent telegram at the ground from my old friend Peter Lorenzo, of the *Daily Herald*, asking me to phone him about the plane crash. He was another who campaigned for my international call-up. When I got to my Essex home at around 3pm after training and saw my wife, she was in tears over the terrible tragedy. She was an avid Manchester United fan and she had heard the news on the radio.

I suppose it was at about that point, once Busby was no longer in charge, that I began to realise that any chance of a Scottish cap had gone for me. I later heard that the committee running the Scottish game were a little snobbish and preferred to use Scottish-based players, or players from more well-known English clubs (unlike little Leyton Orient and Blackburn Rovers in the Second Division) for their World Cup squad.

The Scottish committee decided not to appoint a new manager and it appeared that they did not want to make any changes to the team that had played earlier in the season. Dawson 'Daw' Walker, the man from Clyde, continued as their trainer.

The committee consisted of John W. Park (Queen's Park FC), Robert Kelly (vice-president, Celtic FC), William Waters (second vice-president, St Mirren FC), Thomas Read (treasurer, Partick Thistle FC) and the SFA secretary William Allan. These were the men entrusted with all the teams affairs while in Sweden, including picking the team. The Scots were the only country who didn't have a manager at the competition.

The bulk of the Scottish World Cup squad was made up of players from the Scottish League with a few players from the English League, but to be honest the team never really performed at the tournament. On 8 June 1958 they managed a 1–1 draw against Yugoslavia, on 11 June they suffered a 2–3 defeat against Paraguay (Mudie scored once) and on 15 June came another defeat at the hands of France (2–1). The Scots returned home with very little to show for their efforts. The man who had kept me out of the Scottish World Cup squad in the 1957–58 season was Jackie Mudie.

John Knight Mudie

Blackpool's Jackie Mudie, as he was always known, was born in Dundee on 10 April 1930 and played at junior level with Dunkeld Amateurs and Dunkeld Stobwell. He joined Blackpool from the Lochie Harps club in September 1946 and made his League debut for the Seasiders in March 1950, scoring against Liverpool. In the 1956–57 season he netted 38 goals from 42 senior appearances.

During the following season, when I was breaking all the records with Orient and Blackburn, Mudie was not so prolific, taking just 18 goals from 34 League appearances. He played the latter half of the season as an inside-forward after Blackpool brought centre-forward Ray Charnley to the club.

Mudie was described as an intelligent player with a fast turn of speed who could get up surprisingly high for a short man (he was just 5ft 6½in tall). Mudie was a regular for the Scots in the 1957–58 season and he played at centre-forward in all of their six international matches in that season leading up to World Cup finals in Sweden in June 1958. The Scots had won just twice, drawing three with one loss – a 4–0 defeat by England at Hampden Park. In March 1961, Mudie moved to Stoke City and later played for Port Vale. He had a League career record of 184 goals from 463 appearances. He also ended up with nine goals from 17 Scottish appearances.

Johnny Coyle

The centre-forward cover for Mudie in the World Cup squad in Sweden was Clyde player Johnny Coyle. Although more of an inside-forward he was a prolific goalscorer in Scottish football. In the 1956–57 season, while with Dundee United, he netted 37 senior goals for the Scottish Second Division side. The following season, with Clyde, he scored 20 goals from 21 League appearances. The Scottish team trainer was Daw Walker, who was also the Clyde trainer, and that is how Coyle got into the squad. In fact he never played in the World Cup and never ever won a full cap for Scotland during his career.

My own thoughts

When you look back, the events of the time were really out of my control. On the field, I did as much as I could, hitting six goals while being watched by the selectors. But there was nothing I could do about the Munich air crash ending Matt Busby's short reign as Scottish boss, and the policy of the selection committee. When Busby took charge of a few Scottish games on his return to football, the first thing he did was to drop Mudie. I did then, and still do, think that if Busby had been in charge for the World Cup tournament in Sweden, he would have chosen me at centre-forward with Mudie at inside-forward. I know he admired my style of play. I think Mudie and I would have complimented each other very well. But it never happened and perhaps it was never meant to be.

In hindsight, I am not sure that the move to Blackburn Rovers really enhanced my chances of playing for Scotland. At the time I thought it would – but did it? I certainly helped Rovers gain promotion to Division One, but what if I had stayed with Leyton

Authors' Note: Over the years many good strikers have been chosen to play for Scotland, including: Steve Archibald, Alan Brown, Alan Brazil, Peter Cormack, Johnny Dick, Paul Dickov, Alan Gilzean, David Herd, Mo Johnston, Duncan Ferguson, Dougie Freedman, David Dodds and Joe Jordan. There are some good players there, but Tommy Johnston was superior to most.

In our opinion, only one player in the above list, Alan Gilzean, was in Tommy's class and none of them were as good as Tommy in the heading department. Both Gilzean and Duncan Ferguson were very good in the air, but they could not match Tommy Johnston's ability.

All the players in the list are undoubtedly talented, even if they are not in the same league as Tommy, in our opinion. We think that Tommy ought to have been as well-regarded in Scottish national circles as all of the others were. We have not included in the above listing two of the greatest Scottish post-war forwards – Denis Law and Kenny Dalglish – they were in a class of their own.

We are well aware that many readers may feel that we are over-estimating Tommy Johnston's ability. We think that the reports in the press that mentioned Tommy week in and week out during his career speak for themselves (see Chapter 12).

It is telling that when Jimmy Hill set up a club for international players he invited Tommy Johnston to join. Thus Hill himself and Johnston were the only non-international players of this era among the membership. Maybe Hill was making a statement?

Scottish players with Orient

Orient have had around 30 Scottish-born players on their books since World War

Two. Some gained Scottish caps during their careers with other clubs, but Tommy Johnston was arguably the best of them all, despite his lack of international recognition.

During the pre-World War One years, Clapton Orient, as they were then called, had another great Scottish forward in their ranks, the Cambuslang-born Richard McFadden, who was one of just a handful of truly great Orient forwards in the club's long history. He sadly died in October 1916, during the war, at just 27 years old. Before the outbreak of war he had amassed 66 League goals from his four seasons and he would have hit the 100 mark had he survived. He ranks second to Johnston as one of the top Scottish-born players ever to play for the club.

The Scottish selectors, when debating Tommy's potential inclusion in the squad, might have considered that no Leyton Orient player had ever worn the Scottish shirt at full international level, a situation that was still current in January 2004. Since Owen Williams – the very first Orient player to represent his country and who appeared for England in October 1923 – only 14 players have gained full caps for other countries while on Orient's books. They are: John Townrow, England; Tony Grealish, the Republic of Ireland (Eire); Ciaran Toner, Northern Ireland; Tom Evans, Eddie Lawrence, Malcolm Lucas, Tommy Mills, Ernie Morley and Phil Woosnam, all for Wales; Matthew Joseph, Barbados; Chris Zoricich, New Zealand; and Tunji Banjo and John Chiedozie, Nigeria. They have won a total of 45 caps between them.

Orient? I would certainly have finished on a much higher total than 43 League goals. There was an unsettling period for me just before my move to Rovers; there was the *Daily Express* article which upset me and a few people at Leyton, and that cost me four or five goals at least. Then, there were the eight goals I added for Rovers after the move – surely I would have had 15 or more goals if I had stayed at Brisbane Road? This would have given me a total of around 55 goals, and with a bit of luck I could have even reached the 60 League goals scored by Dixie Dean. With Phil White crossing the ball instead of Bryan Douglas, who was in the Rovers side, anything would have been possible. Douglas was nowhere near White's calibre when it came to delivering an accurate centre, and that was one reason that many felt that Rovers was not the right team for me to join. Perhaps a higher goals total would have convinced the Scottish selectors to pick me, even though I was with Leyton Orient.

The truth of the matter is, we shall never know. Anyway, I had other things on my mind after the Scots returned home from a disappointing World Cup in Sweden during 1958: first, my brother Archie's wedding in July in Arbroath; and second, my First Division debut with Blackburn Rovers at Newcastle United.

Chapter 6

Playing in the First Division, then back to Orient

Despite my disappointment about not being picked for Scotland, at least one of my dreams came true. I played in the highest League in the land when Blackburn Rovers started off in great style in the old First Division.

We went to Newcastle United on 23 August 1958 and beat them 5–1. I scored twice. We played Leicester City on the Wednesday and we beat them 5–0, with one from me. Then it was Tottenham Hotspur at home on the Saturday and we thrashed them 5–0, with another brace from me – then we ended our winning streak with a 1–1 draw at Leicester City. The gates for home matches doubled in size, but the wage packets did not follow suit!

In my first 14 games for Rovers, 11 in Division Two and three in Division One, we scored a total of 59 goals – I wonder if this is some sort of record (I netted 13 of them). It was a good start for us, but then we went to Old Trafford to face Matt Busby's Manchester United and lost 6–1. Things went downhill from then on. Carey kept me in the side, and in December 1959 I bagged a hat-trick against

Newcastle United and scored once in our 4–2 FA Cup win over the Orient. My last game for Blackburn was in the 2–1 defeat at home to Burnley in the fourth round of the FA Cup.

I must admit, I missed the great Phil White's crosses. I had Bryan Douglas to supply me but he was more like a Stanley Matthews type of player and in the end it always seemed to be me laying on the ball for him. He would often dribble to the by-line and pull the ball square while I was waiting for a cross in the middle or on the far post. He was a good player, but we did not combine brilliantly as a partnership. My strength was heading the ball... but Douglas didn't seem to provide opportunities for me.

Just before the home match against Chelsea on 27 December 1958, Dally Duncan (Scotsman Duncan had been appointed boss in October 1958, after Johnny Carey had moved to Everton, taking Roy Vernon with him) called me into his office to show me a letter from a so-called fan which said that Bill Eckersley and I had been in a pub all night before the away match with Chelsea at Stamford Bridge and went back to the hotel roaring drunk. I was furious, as all I had was a glass of drinking chocolate, and then the boss said that he had felt he had to show me the letter. He then threw it in the bin, where it belonged. I suppose the fan was unhappy because we lost 3–0. Maybe the fan that wrote the letter was made a bit happier by the fact that we beat the Blues 2–0 two days later at Ewood Park.

Dally Duncan dropped me at the end of January 1959 and replaced me with Jack Swindells. I became an unhappy man, and as Duncan tried out a number of youngsters in the side, there appeared to be no room for an old 'un like me at Ewood Park. I have always hoped that Duncan's decisions were not influenced by that stupid letter.

Jack Swindells, an England Youth international, only played nine times for Rovers, scoring once. However, he made his mark elsewhere, with spells at Accrington and Workington. He ended his League career with Newport County in 1964 and made a total of 190 League appearances, with 65 goals.

Returning to Brisbane Road

I decided to take action because I knew it was time for me to move on again. I phoned the O's Les Gore one night and asked 'How are you doing, Les?'. He replied: 'Great to hear from you, we're not doing too well. Not playing badly, but we've got nobody to score the goals on a regular basis'. I said 'I know someone at Blackburn who could do a job for you.' He said 'Who?' and I said 'Me'. We chatted for a while and he said he would get back to me.

Les spoke to the O's chairman, Harry Zussman, and they said that they would love for me to return home. So Les Gore made Rovers' manager Dally Duncan an offer, which he accepted, and I gladly returned to Brisbane Road in February 1959 for £7,500. I agreed a wage of £25 per week plus various bonuses.

Stock over-ruled by Zussman

Another little-known fact about my return to Leyton Orient was that manager Alec Stock was very much against my return to Brisbane Road. He was over-ruled by chairman Harry Zussman and he promptly resigned for the third time, so Les Gore was back in charge again. He only returned to management in the summer of 1959 as boss of Queen's Park Rangers, he returned to Orient over the years to sign some of the fringe players like Jimmy Andrews, Mark Lazarus, Derek Gibbs and Malcolm Graham.

The following New Year's Eve me, Les Gore, Nick Collins and all our wives were at Monkhams and Alec Stock and his wife Marjorie popped in and invited us back to their house. I was a bit hesitant about going, but we did, although Marge excused herself and went straight to bed – I think she had been celebrating a bit too well.

There was some tension in the air and my wife Jean piped up. She said: 'For Heaven's sake isn't it time you two stopped sulking at each other'. The air was cleared and Alec said how he was still hurt by that *Express* newspaper article. I explained to him how Roger Malone had twisted the story around. It appears that Alec had really forgiven me after this. At Les Gore's funeral in 1991, Alec was talking to Stan Charlton about the old days at Orient and the camaraderie between the players, and said 'They don't make them like Tommy Johnston anymore'.

Many reporters wrote that I had been no failure in the First Division, scoring 14 times from 25 appearances, yet I was glad to get back to Brisbane Road, having missed Leyton Orient more than anyone knew. Jean and I loved our time there. I got on well with all the lads; they were all friendly and there were no cliques with the players or staff, like there were at some of the other clubs I played with. We moved back to another club house in Buckhurst Hill, Essex.

I must say that, on reflection, I made a very big mistake in moving away from Orient to Blackburn. The way I was going I could have easily got very close to or even broken the long-standing record held by Dixie Dean of 60 League goals in a season.

My return debut was at Fulham on 14 February 1959. We lost 5–2 and I had a shocker, although there was a good reason. Les Gore picked me up from the station on the Friday and we drove to Essex and I got to bed very late. I woke up early the next morning and went straight off to Brisbane Road to sign the papers in time to play at Craven Cottage, where I went straight after completing the paperwork. But despite that shaky start in the game at Fulham, I scored 10 goals in the next 14 games, so the fans couldn't really complain.

The team were in a bit of trouble when I returned, near the bottom of Division Two. Gore had signed the speedster Eddie Brown from Birmingham City and the Cockney man himself Eddie Bailey – so there we were, the three veteran forwards, our ages together totalling 93 years. The three of us gelled very well and things started to pick up for the O's.

200th career League goal
On 21 November 1959 I bagged my 200th career League goal and fittingly it was scored at Anfield. I added a second a few minutes later. Both goals were from crosses from Terry McDonald but unluckily we lost 4–3 to Liverpool. My mate Tommy Younger had

lost his place at Liverpool by then and in goal was another Scotsman, Bert Slater.

I must admit that I didn't know about my achievement until I read it in a newspaper. The club and I should have been more aware of my upcoming feat. Just a few games before, we had celebrated and made a big fuss of Eddie Brown, who achieved his 200th career League and Cup goal with a hat-trick against Middlesbrough at the end of October in a 5–0 win. Brown was a real comedian both on and off the field. He was a very good-natured bloke with a real cheeky personality and was good at upsetting defenders by quoting Shakespeare at them and constantly talking to the fans. I certainly wished I had his tremendous speed.

Why we had forgotten about my upcoming goal milestone I'm not quite sure. It was a big surprise to me when I received a copy of a match report from the *Liverpool Echo*, sent to me in the post by a Liverpool fan and some letters from a few Orient fans congratulating me.

The death of my father and my greatest ever O's goal

I remember 10 January 1960 very well as it was the day my father died. I decided to go home to Loanhead for the funeral and to sort out things with the family. My wife Jean and the kids stayed at home once she found out that traditionally – in my family – only the menfolk attended the funeral, while the women stayed at home.

I learned that my father had died after I returned home from a FA Cup match we played at Liverpool. We lost 2–1 in front of over 40,000 fans. The next day was a Sunday, and we received a message from Les and Amy Gore, who were at the Monkhams public house near our home in Essex. I was told that my brother Jimmy had rung up and left a message asking me to ring him at a certain time at the Roadhouse public house in Loanhead. We had no house phones in those days. When I called him back he told me that my father had died.

I was in Loanhead for a couple of days and my brothers kept telling me how much better my mother was with me there. Then I received a call from my wife telling me that Les Gore wanted me back for the Saturday League match with Huddersfield Town, as they needed the points and would have a far better chance with me in the team. I wasn't ready to go back, and Jean said that if I wasn't coming home she would go and stay with her mother for a while.

Anyway, in the end I decided to go home. Harry Zussman flew me down on the Friday before the game; it took me longer to get home to Essex from Heathrow than it did to fly from Edinburgh to Heathrow. I played at Brisbane Road on 16 January against Huddersfield and scored the winning goal in our 2–1 victory. That one was for my father and I reckon it was the best goal I ever scored for Leyton Orient. The 11,500-odd crowd were very appreciative and I got a rousing reception. The victory was even more satisfying because Huddersfield were on form and had knocked West Ham United out of the Cup the previous Monday evening.

Orient had quite a good season in 1959–60. I started off well with nine goals from eight games and we ended up in 10th position in Division Two, our highest position since returning to that Division. The O's had quite a good record in those days and we were a hard side to beat – no easy meat.

I finished up as top goalscorer again on 25 League goals. To celebrate the club's season, Leslie Grade took all the players, officials and their partners to the Royal Command Performance at the London Palladium Theatre on 16 May 1960. It was a grand show and thoroughly enjoyed by all.

Great goalkeepers

Leyton Orient had a few great goalkeepers on their books when I was with them. The two best men between the sticks were Dave Groombridge and Pat Welton.

David Henry Groombridge was born in Croydon on 13 April 1930. He joined Leyton Orient from Hayes in 1951 but played second fiddle to Welton during the early part of his career. The brave goalie stayed for nine seasons until he had to retire through injury in 1960, making 142 senior appearances.

Roy Patrick Welton was born in Eltham on 3 May 1928, joining the O's from Chislehurst FC in May 1949. He also was with the club for nine seasons and proved to be one of Orient's finest goalkeepers in the post-war era, before he moved on to Queen's Park Rangers in March 1958. He made 281 senior appearances for the O's.

My worst moment in football

I have been asked about my worst moment in football. It was in a League match at Sheffield United in 1959. At that time, they had just introduced nylon studs, and if you walked on concrete, the studs would sharpen like razor blades. I've seen ground staff cleaning boots with those studs and getting their hands cut. We were well into the game when somebody pushed the ball through to me and their goalkeeper Alan Hodgkinson (who was also the England goalie) came out as I ran onto it. He dived across me as I tried to push the ball underneath him and my foot caught his knee. When he didn't get up I went to see what was wrong – he had a cut across his knee and it was sliced open like a peach. I said to him how sorry I was, as I didn't mean to hurt him. This was just before half-time.

During the break, I quickly went into the home dressing room to see how Alan was and their manager Johnny Harris said to me: 'There is no point in saying sorry after you have already done the damage'.

I have never at any time in my career gone out of my way to hurt a goalie, or any player for that matter, so I was stung by the manager's words. I thought Scotsman John Harris, who had a long career with Chelsea between 1945 and 1955 with 326 League appearances, was a top man, but he really went down in my estimation. I later wrote to Alan and told him what had happened and I received a reply telling me that he had no hard feelings, that everything was all right.

This little episode certainly didn't stop Alan from becoming a great goalie. He went on to make 576 League appearances for the Sheffield club between 1954 and 1970, and he earned his fifth England cap in 1961 against Wales.

The best goalkeeper I played with was Ken Nethercott at Norwich and the best I came up against was Reg Matthews, who played over 470 senior games with Coventry City, Chelsea and Derby County between 1950 and 1967.

Third sending-off of my career

On 12 December 1959 I received my marching orders against Scunthorpe United at Brisbane Road. Two of their defenders, Jackie Brownsword and Brian Heward, kept fouling me throughout the game. In the end I just retaliated against Brownsword and that was it, I was gone. Being fouled was nothing new to me – it used to happen every match – but this time I retaliated and I'm not sure why. Brownsword was one of the dirtiest players I played against, but not actually the dirtiest: that distinction goes to Danny Malloy of Cardiff City (see p114 Chapter 10). Brownsword is still to this day Scunthorpe's leading appearance record holder with 597 League appearances. He scored 50 goals between 1950 and 1965, when he was appointed their coach.

I was so incensed about this sending-off that I had a few choice words to say to Scunthorpe's manager Frank Soo. It was obvious that it was their plan to get me out of the game.

Born to an English mother and a Chinese father, Buxton-born Frank Wong Soo played alongside Stanley Matthews and Neil Franklin for Stoke City. The trio also played together for England against Scotland at Villa Park on February 1945. After his playing career ended, Soo coached throughout Europe before returning to manage Scunthorpe for the 1959–60 season. He later went to manage the Israeli national side. He died in Liverpool on 29 January 1991. Frank Soo is known as the forgotten international player, because the FA does not recognise appearances made for England during World War Two. He still is the only player of Oriental descent to have played for England.

My final season with Orient

The 1960–61 season was to be my final one with Leyton Orient. I started off quite well with four goals from the first three games. Then came the first game under lights at Brisbane Road, against Brighton at the end of August. I must admit I don't remember too much about this match. Early on I was kicked in the head by their Scottish-born defender Bobby McNichol. I had to go off – it was quite a cut – but I refused to have stitches and I came on to the field all bandaged up and finished the game. I can't remember much else, but I still have the mark on my head to prove it to this day. So my first League game under lights was special, but for the wrong reasons. I'm told we won the match 2–1.

One of the new members of the O's staff was Matt Busby's son-in-law, Don Gibson. He was a wing-half who played a few games for the O's and made his debut in our 3–1 win at Leeds United, setting up one for me. We got on quite well and the story goes that he left Manchester United because Sir Matt felt uncomfortable picking Don for the team when he and his daughter Sheena starting dating. Don was a good player and he was eventually transferred to Sheffield Wednesday, where he found greater success. Once he brought Sir Matt to Monkhams pub, our local in Essex, to have a drink with Les Gore, Nick Collins, myself and our wives one Sunday evening when he was visiting the Gibsons.

Dropped to the reserves

Our home Second Division fixture against Plymouth Argyle on 26 November 1960 was called off due to a waterlogged pitch. At the age of 33 I had been told I would be rested for the game (dropped more like it) to give youngster Alan Sealey his League debut for Orient. It was our coach, Eddie Baily, who had suggested the switch to Les Gore. Anyway, I then insisted I play for the reserves so I could show old Mr Baily that just because he had retired at the age of 35, there was no need to put me up for retirement as well!

So I played for the reserves against a very strong Chelsea reserves side at Stamford Bridge. They were unbeaten and top of the Football Combination Division One with 12 wins and one draw. They had players like Reg Matthews in goal, Ken Shellito, Stan Crowther, Terry Bradbury, Charlie Livesey, Barry Bridges, Gordon Bolland and Mike Harrison. We also had a strong reserve team out that day: Cochran, Wright, Lewis, Facey, Owen, Sorrell, Waites, Taylor, Johnston, Foster and Sealey. We won 3–2 – I scored, and so did Alan Sealey and Ron Foster. (They were all fine players, but I was the only first-team regular.)

Chelsea's reserves had not been defeated at home very often during the last few seasons. All the Orient first team and officials came to Stamford Bridge to watch us play after their home game was called off.

My marker was Mel Scott, who was being watched for England having played a number of games for the England under-23 side – I gave him the complete run-around. I felt a bit aggrieved at the demotion and I was determined to play extra hard just to prove a point. I had a blinder, making a fool of old Mr Baily. After the match Les Gore came up to me rather embarrassed, but I won't say what he said. Eddie Baily got a few choice words from the boss.

Mel Scott never got his full cap. He joined Brentford in March 1963 and stayed for four years before going to play in the United States in 1967 with the Oakland Clippers. He was picked for the NASL All Star team.

I soon got my first-team place back and played for the following few months, until being 'rested' or dropped again for two League matches in March 1961 so that young Sealey could play. I played in two further reserve games, scoring at Leicester City in a 2–1 defeat on 25 February 1961 and, at home on 4 March against a very powerful Spurs reserve side, I captained the team in a good 2–1 win in which Malcolm Graham scored twice. A subsequent programme report of the game stated that Johnston had a brilliant game, as did young full-back Billy Rennie, whom I had recommended to the club from my old juvenile side Loanhead Mayflower.

I returned to first-team action on 11 March and played alongside Sealey against Luton Town. I set him up with a good chance in front of goal and he back-heeled our winner into the net. This was his final match for Leyton Orient and he joined West Ham United after the two clubs agreed to a swap deal. This resulted in the vastly-experienced centre-forward Dave Dunmore coming to Brisbane Road, and this got me wondering. Big Dave was only 27, and I was seven years his senior – what would happen to me next season?

Anyway, I ended the season on a personal high in April 1961. I scored the goal against my old club Norwich City which kept Orient in the Second Division, much to the delight of the 12,000-odd crowd at Brisbane Road. It was my 17th senior goal of the season.

Then came our visit to Lincoln City, the final match of the season on 29 April 1961. This proved to be my last League game for Leyton Orient. We lost 2–0 in front of a meagre crowd of just 3,996. In goal for that match was Albert Cochran, playing in his only League match. He later became a good friend of mine when he joined me at Folkestone Town.

Carey joins Orient as manager and I'm out of Brisbane Road

In the summer of 1961 came a big turning point in my career. Orient chairman Harry Zussman appointed Johnny Carey (the man who signed me for Blackburn Rovers) as the O's new manager. Carey had just been sacked as the boss of Everton. Les Gore had been offered the position of manager permanently, but he refused it and so Carey got the job, with Gore as his assistant.

The new boss called me into his office and informed me that as I was getting on in years (I was 34 and suffering from a minor injury) he wouldn't be using me as much as they now had Dave Dunmore as a suitable alternative. (Dunmore missed just three games late on in the following season of 1961–62 and scored 22 goals so, in hindsight, I wouldn't have got much of a look-in.)

Carey wanted me to play for the reserve side to bring the young players on and only be called into the first team when I was needed. I was a bit confused by this, as a few months earlier both Ken Facey and myself had been thanked by Les Gore for doing just that with the young reserve lads anyway.

I said to Carey 'Alright, but give me first-team money every week', which at that time was £25 plus bonuses. He said that he couldn't do that, and I would have to be on the same money as the reserve players, at £17 per week. I told Carey 'I can't do what you want me to do, so I'll move on to where I'll be appreciated'. Ken Facey accepted the offer and he stayed with the club for a number of seasons.

Unbeknown to the fans, the first-team players' wages dropped in the summer months to £15. That's why many of them got summer

jobs, like working on a building site or even digging graves. Terry
McDonald knew all about working in a graveyard.

Anyway, Carey informed me that another club had enquired about
me. I asked who was it and he said Gillingham. At the time they were
at the bottom of the Fourth Division. I said to Carey, 'If they'll pay
me the same first-team wages, ring them up and tell them I'm
interested'.

I should have gone to see the Orient chairman and owner of the
club, Harry Zussman, to discuss the proposed drop in wages. I'm
sure he would have reversed Carey's decision. Anyway, I'm a
stubborn Scot and I never did.

It was at this time that I saw Norman Low, my former manager
at Norwich City, at a station. He suggested I go and play in
America. This was a few years before my old mate Phil Woosnam
went over and did a darn good job of it. I decided instead to join
Gillingham. Two former Orient players, Errol Crossan and Len
Julians, did go to play in the States in later years. Crossan went
home to Montreal in Canada after his spell in the US, where he
ended his playing career.

Happy memories

I had such happy times with Leyton Orient. The people I met, the
places we visited and the wonderful times I spent with a great bunch
of players and supporters are all very important to me to this day.
Leaving Orient was the end of a great chapter in my life and as a
player and a man I was very sad it was all coming to a close.

Firstly, I thought of the Leyton Orient supporters; such a special
crowd of people. I remember that after I went to Blackburn Rovers
in March 1958 I was still living in Buckhurst Hill, Essex. I received
an invitation from the O's Supporters Club to attend a Leyton Orient
dinner and Jean and I sat with Les Gore and his wife Amy and Nick
Collins and his wife Doris.

These were the wonderful type of people at Leyton Orient. The
supporters really were marvellous. They presented me with a musical
tankard, which played *Auld Lang Syne,* for breaking the club

goalscoring record in 1957–58. They didn't have to do this, and I had already left them for another club. I was even sadder then about having left them.

The fans were very special. I enjoyed the games of snooker and darts with the fans at Monkhams pub. The players really appreciated the Orient away support and the way they cheered us on at every away match. We players always gave them complimentary tickets when we had them. We often had drinks with them at the many stations we waited at while trying to get home after matches, and their cheering 'Come on the Orient' made us play better. I think now of die-hard fans like Frank Kaye, who was at every away match. They were most certainly a wonderful bunch of people.

My farewell

The Orient programme of 15 March 1958 described the farewell arranged for me by the Leyton Orient Supporters Club at the Chestnut Tree Hotel in Essex. It stated:

> The highlight of the evening was the presentation by yours truly (Mr George Abrahams) of a handsomely engraved tankard to Tommy Johnston from the Supporters Club.
>
> Mention was made of course, to the record goalscoring feats of Tommy whilst with Orient and to the fact of his first few games for Blackburn Rovers. Amid tremendous applause, the tankard was handed over to 'Blackburn's new chum'. Tommy, in a modest speech, thanked the Orient Supporters Club officials and members for their gift which he said would find a place on his sideboard and serve always to remind him of his very happy association with Leyton Orient and all connected with it.

On another page within the same programme, the club was at pains to explain that it was me who wanted to leave. They said that the O's did not want me to leave them, and I was going because I wanted to further my career in the First Division. The piece ended by saying: 'Any player cannot be criticised for doing that'.

Yes, they were good people at Leyton Orient.

The friends we made at Orient

Jean and I made some good friends in football but none more so than 'Mr Orient' himself, Les Gore, and his wife Amy, and Nick Collins and his wife Doris. We used to have a drink with all of them on Sunday evenings. Both Les and Nick were great coaches who got the best out of the Orient players. My friendship with Phil White is well documented (see pp 86 and 115).

Another two blokes I knew at Orient were very good friends of ours, John Short and Bill Jones. Also there was Dave Sexton, the former Orient player and later a good manager, and Jimmy Lee, an O's player who later went to Swindon.

> *Nicholas Collins was born in Newcastle upon Tyne on 7 September 1911. He played many seasons with Crystal Palace, and he joined Orient from Yeovil Town as reserve-team coach during the mid-fifties. He was elevated to first-team coach whenever Les Gore was appointed caretaker manager (frequently!). He left Orient in May 1961 to move to Canterbury. He died during 1990, aged 79.*

Another friend was fellow Scot, Billy Taylor, I went home to Loanhead at the end of July 1959. Les Gore said that he was going to watch some players with a junior team called Bonnyrigg Rose and asked me to join him. This brought back some memories for me, as I had played for my school team on the very same ground.

At the match I said to Les 'That inside-right doesn't look bad' and so it was my job, as Les had to go back to Edinburgh, to see whether the number eight, a lad named Billy Taylor, would be interested in joining the O's. Taylor told me: 'I would go anywhere to play English League football'.

We signed Taylor, and he was a good player and scored a lot of goals for the O's reserves, but he just couldn't quicken himself up. I tried going out with him, having him sprint with spiked shoes on, but he was a one-pace player and nothing helped. He knew the game well and we converted him to a full-back, but after a few games in the O's promotion side and also in the First Division side he lost his place to the more experienced Eddie Lewis and he never got it back.

Billy Taylor finished up going with Johnny Carey to Nottingham Forest when the boss left the club in 1963, and he later successfully coached Oldham Athletic and the England national squad until his early death from complications following a viral infection in 1991.

I have fond memories of my old mate Phil White and his reaction to flying to Malta for a wonderful celebration tour after our promotion to Division Two in May 1956, where I had a good tour with four goals from the three matches.

Phil didn't like flying at all and he said to Les Gore: 'How's about if I go over to Malta on a boat and meet you all there?'. Les Gore turned around to him and said: 'We will have arrived in Malta, played the three games and returned home by the time your bloody boat docks. You will travel with us on the plane'.

I was one who always kidded Phil about his return flight home from Malta. Myself and Johnny Hartburn made a deal with the pilot that the players could come up to the cockpit one at a time. When it was Johnny's turn to go up, I told him to get the pilot to get the plane to tilt a little bit. I was sitting near the window and Phil was sitting next to me and then the pilot tilted the plane and Phil literally turned white. He said 'I think we are going to crash, I want to get off'.

Phil White was my best mate and we were always together.

My time at Leyton Orient was the happiest in my football life, it was such a good friendly club. There were never any arguments and with Harry Zussman and Les Gore you knew where you stood. When I first came from Newport County all the players were friendly and made me feel at home, including Pat Welton, Dave Groombridge, Jack Gregory, Jimmy Lee, Les Blizzard and the skipper and the man who suggested I come to Orient, Stan Aldous.

Harry Zussman

Harry Zussman, the cherubic charmer, was born in Hanbury Street, Brick Lane, London on 24 June 1910. He was the Shoreditch baron of boots and shoes, a natty dresser, and the smoker of a 10-inch cigar

– he kept the Orient afloat for many years along with Leslie Grade. Mr Zussman was a very well-liked man and we were sad to learn of his death in July 1981. I'm told he spent 33 years of his life as chairman and later a director of Leyton Orient and he was devoted to the wellbeing of the club.

Meeting all the famous stars – the wonderful Leslie Grade

During my second spell at Orient I met many film and television stars and some great singers who came to Brisbane Road for home games. One has to remember that the directors, at the time, were Leslie Grade and Bernard Delfont. Their other brother, Lew Grade, was not so involved. It was Leslie who played the major role of the three at the club. It was him, along with the president of the club, Mr F. John Young (although never a director, he supported the club financially between 1948 and 1967), and of course, Harry Zussman, who helped to pay for the team's hotel bills, training camps, tours and holidays.

At the time, the three brothers controlled 80 percent of the British entertainment industry and it was their company, the Associated Television Company, which broadcast on ITV such popular television shows as *The Saint, Danger Man, The Champions, Randall & Hopkirk (deceased)* and *The Prisoner*. They were also involved in many films, including the blockbuster *Jesus of Nazareth* with Robert Powell.

It was not unusual for the stars of the day that appeared at *Sunday Night at the London Palladium* to be brought by Leslie Grade to Brisbane Road on the Saturday. The players were always introduced to these stars before kick-off.

I remember many of them, like the little comedian Arthur Askey (a friendly man, always talking), Shirley Bassey, Ronnie Carroll, Stanley Baker, Tommy Steele, Dave King (who often chatted about betting on the horses), Millicent Martin, Thora Hird and her daughter Janet Scott, and Cliff Richard. Let me tell you, all the heads turned in the stands when the famous actress Sabrina took her seat in the directors' box.

Then there were the international singing stars like Johnny Rae and Pat Boone: Leslie Grade brought them all, he was proud of

Leyton Orient Football Club and he attended every home and many away games with his son Michael.

In January 2004, Michael Grade still remembered Tommy Johnston as the old-fashioned Scottish centre-forward who was good for 25 goals a season and would be worth millions today.

I remember a Saturday match against Aston Villa in February 1960. American singing star Pat Boone was topping the bill at *Sunday Night at the London Palladium* and was brought by Leslie Grade to Brisbane Road. He came into the dressing room to wish us all well. He was wearing a very fancy styled hat and as he was leaving to take his seat in the directors' box, our goalkeeper Dave Groombridge shouted over to him 'Why don't you leave me your hat as a souvenir?' Boone replied that he would, after the match.

He came back to the dressing room after the match, saying how he had enjoyed our performance. He promised to send a hat to each of the players when he got back to the States. Well, he certainly kept his promise, as a month later 17 hats arrived at the club for the players and officials. A cameraman from one of the national newspapers came to take a photograph of us wearing hats from the famous American singer.

We had a very important game against Norwich City on 22 April 1961. Two points were vital to secure our Second Division status. Norwich were pushing for promotion at the time.

I scored the all-important winning goal on 68 minutes and, after the match, the teenage pop idol Cliff Richard popped into the dressing room and congratulated the players on a 'real cool' display. Young Cliff was often seen at Brisbane Road.

Leslie Grade introduced me to a lesser-known personality, Monty M. Berman, the excellent costume designer (not to be confused with Monty Berman, the film producer of the same period). Berman, before his company became so large, was often seen with Grade at Orient home games supporting the boys in the royal-blue shirts.

I had a good friendship with him and often visited his shop in Irving Street, Leicester Square. On one occasion we went next door to his local restaurant for a steak. All the top film stars would pop into his shop for a fitting. It was fascinating to see what he could create, and all the stars that rolled up in their Rolls-Royces.

Monty built up a very large business with offices in Hollywood, Paris, Madrid and Rome. He died on 15 July 2002, when he was 90 years old.

The three brothers, Leslie and Lew Grade and Bernard Delfont have all since died. I'm happy to see Leslie's son Michael Grade CBE is still in the industry, nowadays the owner of Pinewood-Shepperton Film Studios. He still fondly remembers the time he spent with his father watching Leyton Orient.

After I left the O's they won promotion but were struggling badly for survival during the following season in the old First Division.

Leslie Grade went to boss Johnny Carey and asked him how much would it take to save the club from relegation. Carey replied 'Mr Grade, please, don't waste your money'. Carey left at the end of that season with the club back in Division Two.

We were very sad to hear of the death of Leslie Grade in October 1979. He was such a wonderful man and a loyal financial supporter of Leyton Orient Football Club.

Chapter 7

Reluctant move to Gillingham

My long and happy association with Leyton Orient, which was very productive for both of us, was sadly over and I signed for Gillingham on 20 September 1961 for £3,000. I met their boss Harry Barratt and he was open with me. He said what he wanted me to do and I went and did it.

Leyton Orient Football Club kindly placed a nice piece in the club programme about me after I left, which was greatly appreciated. This is what appeared in the Orient programme dated 4 October 1961, after my move to Gillingham:

> I am sure all Orient friends and supporters would wish to pay a tribute to Tommy Johnston, recently transferred to Gillingham FC.
>
> This craggy Scot will go down in Leyton Orient's record books as one of the finest centre-forwards ever to wear the club colours. A consistent goalgetter, with his League tally standing well over the double century mark, Johnston first joined Orient from Newport County. He played a big part in helping O's back into the Second Division after a span of nearly 30 years. He actually scored the goal that won

*promotion. After a move to Blackburn Rovers, the fair-
haired Scot returned to Leyton Stadium in February 1959,
keeping O's out of the doldrums and he did his fair share
in keeping O's in the Second Division.*

*We wish him all the luck in the world at Gillingham and
to him our grateful thanks for his services well and truly
rendered over many years.*

Gillingham were bottom of Division Four at the time I joined them
and really struggling to put any decent results together. I made my
debut against one of the top sides in the Division, Millwall, before
8,205 fans, and scored the opener. We won 3–1, so it was a good
start for me and the match reports said 'Tom Johnston was superb on
his debut'.

I changed my style of play, becoming more of a goal provider than
an out-and-out striker, and I set up quite a few chances for the front
players, Charlie Livesey and Ronnie Waldock.

I remember, during October 1961, we had a trip to Barrow and
would you believe all the other players missed the train at Euston
Station. I was waiting for them, as I had travelled separately from
Essex. Anyway we eventually all got to Gatwick Airport, flew to
Blackpool and caught a few taxis to Barrow, arriving there just in
time for the kick-off. No wonder we lost 7–0.

The team redeemed itself over the following few weeks with two
wins on the trot, first at Carlisle United, where we won 2–1, and
second at home where we had a good win against Colchester United,
another promotion contender. It was 2–1 again and I hit the winner
in front of what turned out to be the largest home crowd of the
season: 8,962. In March, we had another great 4–1 victory over
Carlisle United – they were also title contenders – and I bagged two
goals. The following month I scored against my old club Darlington,
which was pleasing.

Bribery allegations at Gillingham

Over the Easter period in April 1962, we played Wrexham both at
home and away. They were close to a promotion place. I could feel

there was something wrong with a number of our players during these matches and I found out later that four of the players had received £100 each to lose the two matches. We lost 3–0 away and 3–2 at home. One of these players only received half of the money and he was very upset about it. He confided in me about it and gave the names of the other three Gillingham players who had sold the two games against Wrexham. One of the wives also told Jean about it. The whole scandal was reported in the *Sunday People*.

I went to see the chairman, but nothing was really done about it. The FA could not find any evidence against the club or the four players. Soon afterwards Harry Barratt was sacked and a new boss, Freddie Cox, replaced him. As they were all cleared from the allegations, I would never divulge the four players' names.

Harry Barratt is not alive today, Bill Collins is well into his eighties and Dr Grossmark is no longer involved with the club. One of the four players involved has also since died. I just hope that the other three involved, if they are all still alive today, know who they are when they read this, and that the memories start flooding back and they feel very bad about what they did.

I played out the final two League games, but my heart was not in it. The team were safe, nine points clear of the bottom side Chester. I didn't think I could play another season for the club after what had happened with the match-fixing.

Another chapter came to an end as I decided I wanted away from Gillingham. I had scored 10 goals from 36 senior appearances that season. I had done my job and helped get them out of trouble from relegation, so I asked for a free transfer and it was granted.

One of the things I enjoyed about my time with Gillingham was playing with the former Chelsea forward Charlie Livesey. I laid on a few goals for him, we worked well together and it was probably the 25 goals we scored between us that helped the Gills stay up.

On a little fun note, the team went to open a new bowling alley in Gillingham and that was one of my happier moments with the Gills, not playing football but playing tenpin bowling.

Tommy with his father and brothers. Harry, Jimmy, Tommy, Bob (father), Archie, Robert and Alex.

Tommy Johnston in Loanhead as a boy, posing in his brother Archie's uniform.

Tommy (left) and brother Jimmy (second from right) with friends in Loanhead.

Tommy with his father Bob and mother Meg (walking behind) in Arbroath.

Peebles Rovers 1949–1950. East of Scotland Qualifying Cup team. Tommy is in the middle of the bottom row; his brother Harry is second from the right, back row.

Tommy Johnston heads his first goal for Oldham Athletic as he scores the only goal of the game for the Lancashire side against Stockport County. There were 33,450 at Boundary Park that day, 8 March 1952, for a Third Division North match during his brief stay with the Latics.

19 July 1952. Tommy and Jean are married in Oldham by special licence before moving to Norwich.

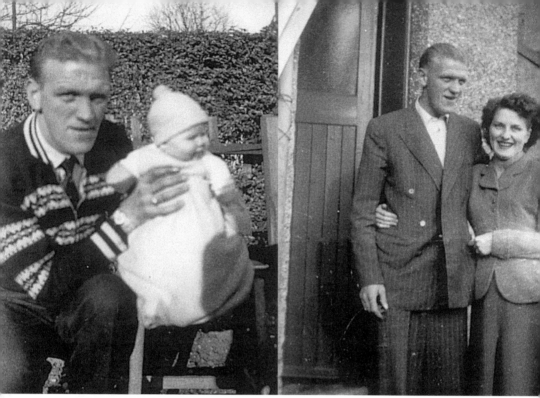

Tommy with Neil, aged three months, in Norwich in 1954.

Jean's first visit to Loanhead in 1952.

Tom did well at Norwich with 33 goals in only 67 games, including both goals in the Canaries' FA Cup win over Arsenal at Highbury in January 1954.

One of Tommy's goals from the January 1954 FA Cup win against Arsenal.

Norwich railway station as the Canaries arrive home after knocking Arsenal out of the cup in January 1954.

With the mayor of Norwich and Vic Oliver, plus teammates.

Tommy Johnston
in action at Carrow
Road during his
spell at Norwich.

A flying header from Norwich's game against Watford on 6
March 1954.

A rare day without any goals. Tommy Johnston in action for Newport County against Northampton Town on 29 September 1955. Town won the game 1–0.

Tommy's Leyton Orient contract.

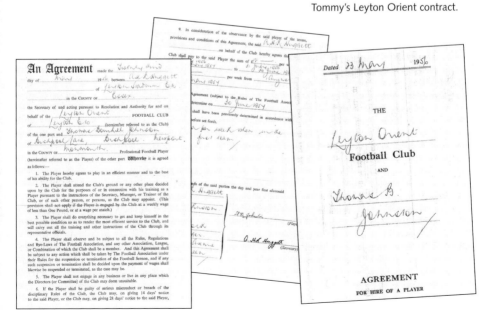

Tommy and his Orient teammates at Saltburn before the match against Middlesbrough on 9 February 1956.

Tommy signing autographs on his home debut for the O's in 1956.

Chapter 8

League career ends, joins Folkestone

So my career in League football came to an end when I left Gillingham. It was not the way I wanted it to end: my pay-out on leaving the Football League was the princely sum of £750, less the income tax. I didn't have a benefit match anywhere, and this little amount of money was all there was to pay tribute to my many years in the professional game. Still, I had all my wonderful happy memories, although I remembered the chat I had all those years ago with old Jimmy Kelly about staying with one club and getting benefit matches.

I left Gillingham to go down to Southern League side Folkestone Town and was signed as player-coach by their manager Wilf Armory, a Geordie, on 6 July 1962. We got along fine. I remember the man swam in the English Channel every morning between March and October!

Injured in car crash

Before I played a single match for my new club, I was involved in a terrible car accident. The accident occurred while we were still living in Gillingham. An acquaintance named Albert asked if I would like

> *Wilf Armory was born in Crook on 23 January 1911. He was an inside-forward in his playing days with Crook Town and Ayr United, with whom he made nine Scottish League appearances in the 1930–31 season. He returned south of the border to join Aldershot in 1932, playing just a few games before joining Nuneaton Borough. He was something of a legend with Folkestone, having been with the club since April 1934. He later became a much-admired and respected manager between 1942 and June 1975, later becoming both a director and club president until his death on 21 December 1996, which ended a 62-year association with the club. The Wilf Armory stand is still around even today, to ensure that he is never forgotten.*

to go and watch Kent play country cricket in Dover. I told him that I had to go to Folkestone first to sign my contract for Folkestone Town with Wilf Armory.

He said that was fine and that would he would run me down to Folkestone first and then carry on to Dover. I met with Wilf and signed the contract, so officially I was a Folkestone player. We all had a quick cup of tea and then headed for Dover.

I was sitting in the front of the car with Albert, who was driving, and there was one other passenger, named John. Everything was fine then we reached the main Dover road; it was now mid-morning. The next thing we knew, a vehicle from the opposite direction came straight for us, and then 'bang'. There were no seat belts in those days. I was flung out of the car, and hit my head very hard on the side mirror. I sustained a half-circle wound on the top of my head and also injured my knee, ankle and foot.

The driver, Albert, had six broken ribs, but our back-seat passenger was just shocked. We were all taken to Dover hospital. My head was stitched up and I was told that I might have to have ligament surgery on my leg. When I arrived home, all my clothes were covered in blood. I still have the scar on my head from the accident. My biggest fear at the time was that I would not be able to head a ball again, but eventually it healed and it was alright.

It was literally just a few minutes after I had signed the contract with Folkestone that the accident occurred. I hate to think what would have happened if the accident had occurred just before I put pen to paper.

Jean and I rented a club house in Gillingham, which was owned by one of the directors, just down from the Central Hotel, where I recuperated from the accident. It was at this time that my former Orient colleagues were preparing for their campaign in the First Division. I thought as I was moping around the house that it would have been nice to be with them and a part of all the hype. I felt happy for people like Les Gore, Harry Zussman, the Grade brothers and players like captain Stan Charlton, Sid Bishop, Eddie Lewis and of course my old mate Phil White, but I was sorry not to be part of it any more.

Due to my injuries, I missed out on playing in Folkestone's three FA Cup qualifying matches. The first was against Canterbury City, which we won 3–0, before going out to Sittingbourne after a replay.

Booed and jeered by the Folkestone fans, but soon I become their hero
When I returned to match action, I started off in bad fashion, having still not fully recovered from the car accident. This was not very well reported in the local Folkestone press and when I did return, I was not at all at my best. I remember being, well, not so popular at Cheriton Road and I was even given the bird as I walked from the pitch after the first few matches with the crowd shouting at me 'Try harder!' and 'Too slow!'. Once they heard about the accident, they became much more sympathetic. Eventually everything came good but it took a lot of hard training.

I just got on with what I was doing at Folkestone. It felt a little strange down on the coast and it took me a while to settle down after the accident. We had a large number of old ex-League professionals in the squad, and once we all gelled together, the team did well. In my first season we finished as champions, getting up to the Premier Division of the Southern League. It was a wonderful achievement in my first season as player-coach.

It was during this period that the 'big freeze' took place and we missed about seven weeks of football, which gave me a bit more time to get fit. I had something to prove to this lot and I trained very hard to get back to match fitness. During March 1963, I gradually found my touch and began to score goals again, knocking in 11 goals in four Southern League games to become, yet again, the fans' hero. I felt good again.

Manager Armory told the local press: 'I just knew Tommy would eventually confirm my faith in him, he has knitted the team together and has brought the best out of the players in the team and has led the revival of the club.'

We needed a goalkeeper and I recommended we sign Leyton Orient's Welsh-born goalkeeper Albert Cochran, who had been languishing in the reserves, having made just a single appearance in the first team at Lincoln City in April 1961, which also happened to be my final appearance for Orient. He joined us in May 1963 and stayed for a number of seasons as the first-choice goalie.

The following season, we did quite well and finished in 10th spot in the Premier Division of the Southern League. Now that I was getting on in years, I decided to play in a much deeper role and to try and lay on goals for Tony Biggs and the other forwards.

We had a good little run in the FA Cup up to the first round proper, having beaten Sheppey at home in the second qualifying round by 2–0, Ramsgate away by 3–1 in the third qualifying round and then Ashford Town 3–0 at home in the fourth qualifying round.

I would have played in these games, but for an injury I sustained in a home pre-season friendly against Leyton Orient on 17 August 1963. I sprained my tendon rather badly and I had to go to hospital for an X-ray.

The match ended 2–2 but I left the field early on and didn't find the net. I played my first game of the season that September in a Metropolitan reserve match against Margate and came back into the first team only in October when I played against Trowbridge, in a Southern League Division One match on 26 October 1963.

My last big career game, in the FA Cup at Oxford United

Then came my last big game in football. It was in the first round proper of the FA Cup at Fourth Division Oxford United. We thought we had a good chance as it was only their second season as members of the Football League, but we lost 2–0. The match took place on Saturday 16 November 1963 in front of 7,294 spectators and our team that day was: Cochran, Wilson, Anderson, Peplow, Patrick, Tredwell J., Ireland, Churms, Biggs, Johnston and Legate. Many of these were former League players.

Two regulars in the side were former Leyton Orient players. Albert Cochran was in goal, and up front, playing in my former role as an attacking centre-forward, was my old mate Tony Biggs. Both Cochran and Biggs stayed with Folkestone for a number of years, enjoying much success. Biggs also proved to be a fine header of a ball.

I remember the club arranged a charity match against a Showbiz XI side to celebrate our good season and a few of the pop and film stars were there. One of them, Tommy Steele, springs to mind. After the match, we were invited to have some refreshments with them. I wanted to go straight home but the wife refused as our daughter Alison adored the young pop star. She ran up to him and flung her arms around his neck and gave him the biggest hug and kiss you could imagine – Tommy Steele took it all in good fun.

I was full-time with Folkestone. I was going down to the ground every day and cleaning out the dressing rooms and baths. I then trained with the players twice a week, but I was getting the same money, £25 per week, that I got with both Leyton Orient and Gillingham. The menial work was something new to me but I had to get on with it because at least I was earning a decent wage.

The end of the road?

I left Folkestone when one day I was called in by the chairman and told they couldn't afford my wages anymore. I thought to myself 'fair enough', and I decided to retire from football. I had played for 15 years and spent the last year as a coach, and it was the end of the road. In more recent times people have tried to get details of my playing record with Folkestone Town, but all the records were lost during changes at the club. I believe that today they are called

Folkestone Invicta. Anyway, in May 1964 I left them after two happy seasons and moved north.

The club had a nice bunch of supporters and one lovely touch was that the Folkestone Supporters' Club presented me with a tankard on a farewell night they arranged for me, which was inscribed 'To Tom Johnston – To The Master'. Jean was presented with a beautiful bouquet of flowers. This was all arranged by Tommy Scannell, the ex-Southend United goalkeeper, who had retired to Folkestone at the time. Scannell was a very nice man, and he nicknamed me 'the master' because of my ability on the ball. The name stuck while I was with Folkestone and that's why it was engraved on the tankard.

When we revisited the UK in 1989 we paid Tommy Scannell a visit and he was still the same man, a delightful Irishman. However, he died a couple of years later. His son was Sgt Roach in the television programme *The Bill*, but we never met him.

Moving up north

We left Folkestone as soon as we had sold the house, which happened very quickly, and we moved up north and settled in before applying for a licence for the betting shop, which we opened up in November 1964, at Poulton-le-Fylde, three miles outside Blackpool. The shop was called Tom Johnston Bookmakers (Ltd). We had financial help from my wife's oldest sister and her husband, who became partners in the business.

One last fling

Then I got a call from the player-coach of Lytham St Annes FC, of the Lancashire Combination League, a Les Rigby, who asked if I wanted to play and coach for them. We met in a public house and I signed for them in October 1965, making approximately 10 appearances.

The money I got helped to pay my brother-in-law to work on a Saturday in the betting shop. I was quite happy with that, and I enjoyed my brief run-out with Lytham St Annes.

I applied for the player-manager's position with Fleetwood, but they wanted me just to manage the team. I thought it would be of benefit to them if I played as well, but I turned the job down anyway.

I was asked to sign on for a further season with Lytham St Annes. After a good think about it, I decided to pack it in. At the age of nearly 39, it was getting harder to keep fit and keep up with the youngsters, even in training, and anyway we were thinking about going to Australia.

Chapter 9

Move 'Down Under'

We left the shores of England on Monday 3 January 1972 and arrived in Australia two days later. After all the years of trying, the family had finally emigrated to Oz and settled in a little town called Dapto at 4 Laver Road. This house was not far from the bus stop and station, and after a while I had to go to work in Port Kembla and Jean had to go to Figtree to her job at K-Mart.

One of the first things we had to do was learn to drive a car. Soon after that we got a second-hand station wagon, mainly to get our son Neil to university as transport was very lacking in the country areas. When Neil managed to save enough money to put down a small payment on a car, we took over the old station wagon and drove it around.

My wrist was playing up at that time and I went to see a Dr Sweeney, a plastic surgeon who came to Wollongong once a month from Sydney, to ascertain whether he could reduce the bulkiness of the original surgery done in 1945. He was able to do this and he was also fascinated by the original surgery and asked who did it. We told him and he was amazed, saying that they had served in the army together at the end of the war.

After only the first week or so, I found out that my old Killie manager Alex Hastings was living in Melbourne. After running a hotel, pub and a bookstore in Scotland, he had emigrated to

Australia in 1965 and become the president of the South Australia Soccer Federation.

I rang him up to ask him about the game of football in Australia and he said 'don't touch it'. He said that the game had too much politics and I appreciated his advice. He suggested that I try to get a coaching job with a works team, and that's exactly what I did. Soon after we arrived, I saw an advert in a local newspaper for a coaching position at John Lysaghts, an old British company from Bristol, who were manufacturers of various corrugated products and located in Port Kembla in New South Wales. I went to see a Mr Ellis Bridge on 14 February and I got the job. He asked if I had a job outside of football. I said I hadn't yet, so he also found me a job as an inspector with the electricians and fitters at Lysaghts.

The coaching job didn't pay much, but with the inspector's job and with Jean working at K-Mart, the family was alright financially. I advertised for local players to attend our first training session and only three turned up: Stevie Lawler, my son Neil, and a Greek lad named George, so I also signed up as a player. Eventually I put a team together and we did alright.

In my first season, at the age of 44½ years old, I was playing for the reserves along with my son Neil and we scored nearly all the goals. I got 15 and Neil ended up on 16 goals. I coached the team for a couple of years, but I did fill in a few times when we were short of players. One of the best results we had was a win over the local Yugoslav side Primbee and it was quite an upset in the history of local football.

I started playing golf and snooker again after my football career came to an end during late 1974. After suffering a serious neck injury at work, I accepted an average compensation payout and retired in 1988 at the age of 61. I had many happy times at John Lysaghts, and they gave me a very nice Citizen watch for service, which I still have to this day.

A holiday to the UK
In 1989, Jean and I went on holiday to the UK and we went straight

to Loanhead to stay with my nephew Tom (he was named after me) and his wife Isobel. While in Scotland we went to quite a few football matches. One was to visit my former Blackburn colleague Ally McLeod, who was boss of Ayr United. They were playing Alloa Athletic. We were invited into their boardroom, and Jean was the very first lady ever to be invited into that sacred Ayr boardroom. Ally McLeod died on the morning of 1 February 2004 at his home in Ayrshire at the age of 72 after suffering from Alzheimer's disease. He led the Scottish side to the 1978 World Cup finals in Argentina. In July 2003 he received an award for his services to the Scottish national side and to football in general. Having devoted his entire life to football, he will be sadly missed.

We then travelled to Oldham to stay with Jean's cousin Joan and visit old friends. Then we went back down to Folkestone to stay with friends, Brenda and Dave Foreman, and visit the Cochrans before moving on to Essex.

Jean and I were met in London by our old mate John Short. We stayed in a lovely bed and breakfast in South Woodford and met up with all our friends from both inside and outside of football and John took us everywhere.

Meeting Sir Matt Busby

Another wonderful moment for us was when we visited Sir Matt Having spent a day out in Manchester, we decided to visit Old Trafford. Matt was kind enough to fit us into his very busy schedule and it was a wonderful chance to be with the great man and talk about old times and old players. We had about 30 minutes with the great man before he had to go to a meeting with Bobby Charlton, so we didn't have much time to talk. He left and we then went to have lunch at Lou Macari's fish and chip shop. We were both so sad to have heard of the death of Sir Matt Busby on 20 January 1994 in Manchester.

Back to Brisbane Road after 28 years

The trip culminated in our final port of call on 14 October 1989, and a great day was had at Brisbane Road. This was my first trip back to Leyton Orient for 28 years, and it was as the guest of honour of their Vice-Presidents' Club. We watched the O's beat Blackpool 2–0, and during half-time I presented one of their star players, Steve Castle, with a trophy for a previous man-of-the-match award. I think I signed more autographs that day than throughout my entire Orient career. It brought back many wonderful memories for Jean and me, and it was nice to meet the O's supporters in their clubroom and to see some of my former Orient colleagues like Sid Bishop, Terry McDonald, Joe Elwood and Phil McKnight.

After a wonderful stay in the UK, John Short took us back to Heathrow and we left for a two-day stopover in Singapore before returning home. We have since lost touch with John Short.

The trip was an illustration for me of why I loved playing football for a living, especially with Orient. Twenty-eight years after leaving Leyton Orient I'm still fondly remembered by the O's fans. It was a lot better than working down the coal pit! Playing football was the easy way out for some of us Scottish lads; working down the mine was hard graft, as I know only too well.

Chapter 10

On reflection

The best players I've ever played with in my long career would have to be Phil Woosnam and Phil White of Leyton Orient. Mention is made, later in this chapter, of my wonderful partnership with Phil White but, as for Phil Woosnam, he was the best of them all. He was a really terrific young player with Orient. He had skill and vision beyond his young years and he fully deserved the stardom that he later attained playing for West Ham, Aston Villa and Wales, winning 17 caps during his career before taking the game to America. It's well documented what great work he did and is still doing at all levels of soccer in the US.

Inside-left Noel Kinsey was one of the best players I had played with at Norwich City. He was one of the all-time great forwards for the Canaries with 65 goals from 243 senior appearances. He later had a good spell with Birmingham City and Port Vale, and he also played seven times for Wales.

Johnny Summers was a great friend of mine and also a top-quality classy forward. He was born a month later than me in September 1927 and had a wonderful career with a number of southern-based clubs including Fulham, Norwich, Millwall and Charlton Athletic, making a grand total of 338 League appearances and scoring 173 goals. Sadly, he died at the young age of 37 on 2 June 1962, at the same time I was joining Folkestone.

There were also two other good friends of mine who were both really excellent but little-known players, whom I played with at Kilmarnock. These were Alex Donaldson and Jimmy McGill.

Donaldson, like me, was born during 1927. He made his Killie debut in October 1949 and played 79 senior games, scoring 25 goals. After a spell with Buckie Thistle in the Highlands League in December 1952, he went to England to play for Kettering Town in August 1953. He never played in the English League. I'm still in contact with Alex, who today lives in Ontario, Canada.

Outside-right Jimmy McGill was born in Kilsyth, Scotland during 1926 and was with Bury after the war. In March 1947 he moved to Derby County, making seven League appearances before joining Killie in October 1949 for cash, along with a player named Hugh McLaren. McGill made just 20 appearances for Killie, scoring three goals before going on to good things with two top-flight teams at the time, Berwick Rangers and Queen of the South. He ended his career with Cowdenbeath in 1953.

Come to think of it, that would be a really great forward line... White, Woosnam, Johnston, Kinsey and Donaldson, with McGill and Summers both waiting in the wings as reserves.

I must make mention of one of the forgotten men at Leyton Orient: Len Julians. I suppose it was mainly my fault that he was left out of the side so much. When I was scoring all my goals he never got a decent run in the side. Julians netted 69 reserve goals for the club. When we did play together, we worked very well and he netted 16 goals in the 1957–58 season.

Funnily enough, he never quite performed for the club after I left for Blackburn and made just 68 senior appearances during his four seasons with the club. He was eventually sold to Arsenal for £12,000 in December 1958. He then moved on to Nottingham Forest and Millwall, and it was while with the Lions that he came good, scoring 58 goals from 125 League appearances. Len died in Southend-on-Sea on 17 December 1993, aged 60.

The best managers I played for

Mention is made in the various chapters on my career about the managers I have served over the years. I don't have to think too hard about who I consider the best I served under: it was definitely Les Gore. He was a wonderful man and a great manager and loyal servant to Leyton Orient. During his time at the club he was in charge for 187 League games with 79 wins, 40 draws and 68 losses. Goals scored totalled 301, with 289 against, with 198 points obtained.

Alec Stock was a decent man and had a good career in management. His only fault, in my mind, was that he tried to change my style of play. However, there is no doubt that Stock was one of the game's legendary managers. Born in Peasedown St Johns, near Bath, Somerset, on 30 March 1917, he had a wonderful 34-year managerial record and over 1,000 matches with Yeovil, Orient (three times), QPR, Luton Town, Fulham and AFC Bournemouth. He died in Somerset on 16 April 2001 aged 84.

As for Johnny Carey, he didn't say very much to the players other than a short chat in the dressing room as a pre-match talk. In the 1961–62 season he took Leyton Orient to promotion up to the old First Division.

The other outstanding managers I played under were Alex Hastings at Kilmarnock and Billy Lucas at Newport County. So in my mind these three – Les Gore, Alex Hastings and Billy Lucas – were without doubt the best. They always sorted out problems at team meetings. They also had faith and left it to the more experienced players to sort things out on the field of play.

As far as I'm concerned, managers should only advise you how to play as they have no idea how the other side is going to play in any given situation. These three men let me play my way.

The dirtiest player I ever played against

Apart from Jack Brownsword of Scunthorpe United (mentioned in Chapter 6 in regard to my third sending-off) I would have to say the dirtiest player I have ever played against was Danny Malloy, the

Cardiff City centre-half. I played against him a few times for both Orient and Blackburn Rovers, and he would be forever kicking the back of my legs. I would spend half of the following week in the treatment room, hoping to get fit for the next match. It was alright though, as I scored a few against him.

> *Malloy was born in Dennyloan on 6 November 1930. The rugged 25-year-old joined Cardiff City from Dundee in October 1953 for £17,000. He played 72 League games in succession and was a Scotland 'B' international. He stayed with Cardiff for five years, making 225 League appearances, scoring once. He moved to Doncaster Rover as player-coach-manager in October 1961 and played 42 League games. He returned to Scotland in the 1962–63 season to join Clyde.*

My thoughts on Phil White

Before I start, I must say that Phil and I struck up a good friendship straight away. We both liked the same things like dog racing, horse racing and snooker. I could kid him about anything and the thing was, he always believed everything I said.

Phil White was a great right-wing man and the two of us just gelled. He was a terrific crosser of the ball: you almost knew that the ball would finish up in the back of the net. It was almost telepathic, the understanding between us, and we were just top-class together. In fact, you could say we were made for each other football-wise.

White's crosses came over at just the right speed and right angle. His crossing ability was rare and he always maintained a consistent level. It was a pity that we didn't get the chance to play together at the highest level, but this did not diminish our achievements and ability.

Once, when we were playing at Lincoln City, Phil was admiring the camel coat of director Leslie Grade and Grade told White that if he scored a hat-trick, he could have the coat. Quick as a flash White replied, 'Would it be OK if my mate scored them?' (meaning me).

In a previous chapter I mentioned Phil's hatred of flying, and he was a worried man when he heard Harry Zussman and Leslie Grade had arranged a tour to Malta to celebrate our promotion in May 1956. Phil was so scared as we approached the time to leave that, a few weeks before, he got a so-called bad sore throat, in the hope that the club doctor would say he couldn't travel. The doctor just gave him a gargle, and everyone knew it was just Phil's nerves.

It was a great tour and we think Phil enjoyed it. In 1960 we went on tour to Jersey and the players had strict instructions: 'Don't tease Phil about the flight'.

Bill Robertson, the former Chelsea and Orient goalkeeper, who like Phil also lived in West London, told me a story after I had left the club:

> Once the O's had to fly on a plane to go on tour and you should have seen Phil. The plane was caught in one of those wind pockets and it was pouring down with rain and poor Phil was going off his head and he started performing, shouting 'get this plane down and get me out of here!'.

About 30 minutes before every home match when we were all playing, Phil, Ken Facey and myself would tell Les Gore we were going to Alice Underwood, the tea lady, for a cuppa, but instead we all went to have a quick smoke. If Les only knew!

I remember a match we played at West Ham United and Irishman Noel Cantwell was their left-back. Phil was told by Les Gore to pass the ball before the Irishman got anywhere near him. I told Phil instead to take the ball to him and go past him, as if he wasn't there. Phil did just that. Poor old Cantwell, he got quite frustrated and at half-time he came over to me, as he must have heard me talking to Phil, and said 'You play your game and let him play his'. He was a top-quality defender who won 36 caps for Eire during his long career of over 360 League appearances with both the Hammers and Manchester United and he was being totally outplayed by Phil White.

Phil was quite surprised when he heard that Liverpool had put in an offer for him of £15,000 to the Orient board. He asked me, 'Do they have a dog track?' and jokingly, 'Where is Liverpool, anyway?'. He told Les Gore that he was not at all interested in leaving Orient. He was a true Orient man through and through.

Phil loved his poached eggs. For every evening home game, he would travel from his south London home to me in Essex. We would very briefly, for just a few seconds, discuss our tactics for the match and, more importantly, we would have poached egg on toast before we travelled together to Brisbane Road on the underground. We walked and talked while walking down Leyton High Road to the ground. When I returned from Blackburn Rovers for my second spell with Orient, I walked into the dressing room. We were playing at Fulham and Phil was pleased as punch to see me again, as I was to see him. He turned to Eddie Baily and said 'You can keep quiet now, the boss is back'.

I remember the Royal Command Performance in May 1960. Before the start of the evening, comedian Bud Flanagan came onto the stage to give the audience a few pointers on etiquette in front of the Queen. One rule was that you were to remain seated throughout the show in the presence of Her Majesty.

Halfway through the show Phil turned to me and whispered 'I have to go to the toilet'. I replied 'just go, she can't stop you'. Now poor old Phil decided to wait, but near the end of the show I could see it was all getting too much for him and I said 'come on, I'll go with you'. We both quietly sneaked out, only to find that there were plenty of people in the foyer queueing for the toilet anyway.

During our tour to the Channel Islands, Phil kept asking me to check out his knees because he thought he had sustained an injury. Everyone was saying he was fine and there was nothing wrong. He was right though, one knee looked much more swollen than the other one and on his return to London he went to see a specialist and went in for an exploratory operation, ending up having his cartilage removed. Anyway, it all turned out well and he was back for the new season.

Regarding Phil's crosses, I would not really have a clue where the cross would be after Phil got the ball on the wing. I would make a beeline for the goalmouth, it was just a natural thing, and the ball would be in the box for me. I trusted our Phil to get it over for me to head at goal.

In closing, Whitey was a top man and a top player. We also had a really good friendship off the playing field, and we were always together when on tour in Malta or in the Channel Islands. In most of the photographs taken of the Orient players either on tour or at one of our training camps you will notice we are always seen together.

After moving to Australia, we exchanged Christmas cards every year with Phil right up to his death in 2000. It was quite uncanny; two other former O's colleagues of mine, whose surnames also began with the letter 'W', died in the year 2000 – George Waites and George Wright.

> *Philip George John White was a loyal Orient man, born in Fulham on 29 December 1930. He came to Brisbane Road from Wealdstone FC in 1953 and stayed for 11 seasons, making 233 senior appearances, scoring 28 goals and being rewarded with a testimonial in 1964. This came after he had to retire owing to a long-term injury.*

Authors' Note: Top-quality goalscorers are worth their weight in gold to any club but so are quality goal-makers – in Phil White, Leyton Orient had the perfect foil for Tommy Johnston, who allowed him to set his many club records.

Today's modern game is woefully short of good crossers of a ball. No wonder David Beckham, the former Orient junior, looks so good and the rest are so poor in this respect. Beckham's centres are very accurately placed, but often they are too flat. Phil White's were just beautiful centres and ideal for any would-be strikers, and he was so consistent. We would say that the top three crossers of a ball in the modern game are White, Dave Thomas (QPR and Burnley) and David Beckham (Manchester United and Real Madrid).

Tommy Johnston was a great player. He headed in goals from crosses from Baily, Brown, Elwood, Facey, Hartburn, McDonald and Jimmy Smith. So he didn't really need Phil White to make him great, but when the two were playing together, well it was near perfection.

In the early days of their partnership, they just murdered the opposition. On 17 March 1956 when the O's thrashed Aldershot 8–3, these two destroyed the Soldiers' defence with Phil Woosnam prompting superbly. White made six of the goals and Johnston bagged a hat-trick and was unlucky not to have scored two more.

The O's fans became accustomed to the great understanding of this duo, and even three seasons later they were still doing their thing. The 5–0 drubbing of Middlesbrough during October 1959 was a tremendous classy team display from

Orient and all that was missing was a Johnston goal. One can never forget the way that Tom and Phil put the icing on the cake – it nearly brought the house down – some White magic on the right and a scorching Johnston header to finish it off majestically, terrific stuff.

White's crosses were always accurate, even if he delivered them from very awkward positions and tight situations and got them into the ideal position for Johnston to score from. He was also an excellent dribbler and the word 'bamboozled' was used in many a match report in describing his mastery over full-backs and defenders.

There can be no doubt that the Johnston-White partnership was a high-class combination. There was always a level of expectancy when White had the ball on the right wing and Johnston was waiting in the middle. When these two players were in the O's team you knew Orient were in with a chance of winning, whoever the opponents were.

With players like Phil Woosnam, Stan Charlton, Ken Facey and Sid Bishop in the side at around the same time, Leyton Orient should perhaps have achieved more than they actually did. The duo were a joy to watch and in the later stages of the 1958–59 season they caused havoc among opponents' defences.

Very few combinations worked together for Orient so well. Some who did well were McFadden and Dalrymple before World War One, Facey and Rees in the early 1950s, and Kitchen and Mayo in the 1970s, but none could really compare.

Fittingly the last time Tommy Johnston played at Brisbane Road was when he appeared for an ex-Leyton Orient XI against the O's first team on 21 April 1964. It was Phil White's testimonial match, which was drawn 3–3. Johnston scored a goal from the penalty spot – he was the Folkestone Town player-coach at the time.

Chapter 11

Thoughts of a footballer's wife

They say that behind every good man, there's a great woman. Well, Jean Johnston has certainly shown this to be true, sticking by her man and travelling around the country and moving into a number of club houses while her husband Tommy played professional football and lived his dream. They also say, that to find out the truth about any man, you ask his wife, so that's exactly what we did when we asked Jean Johnston to tell her story. We also spoke to their children Alison and Neil. These are their memories of Tommy in their own words, starting with Jean.

I was born Jean Waite at 74 Fisher Street, Oldham, Lancashire, the middle child of Helena and Charlie Waite, and had a happy childhood. I was a football fan a long time before I knew Tommy Johnston, and I watched the local side Oldham Athletic with my father when I was about 14 years old. As I got a little bit older my cousin Joan Waite, my friend Mavis Dawson and I went to watch

Oldham and were friendly with the majority of the players, whom we met at social functions.

Religion played an important part in my early life, and I was baptised and confirmed in the Church of England. I went regularly as a young girl with my cousin Joan; we were buddies. During the years when we didn't have very much money we made some wonderful friends being in the local choir. A group of six of us stayed friends for many years and it certainly gave us a foundation for being ethical and honest.

How I met Tommy

I met Tommy on 1 April 1952 at a sports night for the Oldham players and their supporters. At that time Tommy had only been with them a few months. I probably wouldn't have been there – we normally went dancing – but I was just recovering from an appendix operation and my Dad decided I really shouldn't go dancing so I went with a friend of mine to this sports night and that's when I first met Tommy.

Prior to meeting Tommy I worked in a cotton mill called Abraham Stotts cotton mill. After the war, and the bleak period that went with it, everything sort of came alive and we had lots of stage musicals and we went dancing. It was really a bright and happy time. The cotton queen contest was revived throughout all the cotton mills in Oldham and I was chosen as the cotton queen for the mill in around 1949. I became a photographer's model – clothes on, I might add – and did many photographs for the studio.

From there, I won quite a few beauty queen pageants including Miss Devon Coast Country Club and the Oldham Cinema Queen. It didn't cost Tommy anything to take me to the cinema – I won a free pass for the whole year! Once we moved to Norwich, we lost the benefit.

From then I was trained to be a fashion model and my pictures were sent to Granada Television prior to their opening with a view to advertising products or being a future show hostess. The new station was in the early stages of development and its television service was being planned.

So I met this man named Tommy Johnston, a big blonde Scot, a very shy man and we started going out together. Then he went off home to Loanhead for a week, but we then teamed up again when he returned to stay at lodgings with Mr Bill Ludlam, the Oldham reserve-team trainer.

Tommy's best friends at Oldham were fellow-Scot Bill Ormond, an inside-forward from Greenock, who played 122 games for Oldham, scoring 24 goals and later playing for both Barrow and Scunthorpe; and Orig Williams from North Wales, a reserve player, who was released at the same time as Tommy.

We get married in July 1952

Tommy signed for Norwich City and asked me if I would go with him. At that point in time I had no intention of getting married as I had my modelling and a possible television career looming.

However, I did decide to marry Tommy and we got a special licence on the Monday and we married on Saturday 19 July 1952. Our best man was Bill Ludlam, and Orig Williams was also at our wedding.

We then went off to Scotland to collect the rest of Tommy's things and to meet his family, then we went back to Norwich. We lived in digs for a couple of months and then we moved into a large house in Grove Road in Norwich, which we shared with Ken Oxford and his wife Joan; they lived downstairs and we lived upstairs. There wasn't one lock on any of the doors and it really was a good job that we got on very well with the Oxfords.

In the summer, we had our first holiday in Great Yarmouth. It was nice just to be together.

We moved into a house in Brian Avenue in Norwich, which had previously been occupied by former Canaries player South African-born Alf Ackerman and his family. (Ackerman was a hard man, being rather tough on the younger Norwich players during training.)

Tommy was quite a natty dresser, especially after being told off at Norwich for attending training without a tie. It was 80-degree heat at the time and he was warned that if it happened again, he would receive a five shillings fine. He made sure it never did.

When our son Neil came along we had a little bit of an anxious time. We had no telephone in the house; we had only moved in about five weeks before. I was hundreds of miles away from my family and I was in the last throes of giving birth to this baby.

I made friends with the lady next door and she said that I should bang on her door in the middle of the night if anything happened as Tommy had gone away to play for Norwich City. For some strange reason, they had two away games, which was quite unusual over the Christmas and New Year weekends. It was normal to have one of the festive season games at home.

Neil was due on 28 December and Tommy left his phone number everywhere but in the end Neil Thomas Johnston was born on Monday 4 January 1954, in a place called Drayton Hall, about five miles outside of Norwich.

Well, as you can imagine at that time of the year it was very cold, with snow and ice. Tommy, who got home in the early hours of that Sunday morning after a match, had to cycle on the icy roads to Drayton Hall to visit me and his new son. I returned home 12 days later.

Tommy comes home with a bunch of sausages

Soon after Neil's birth Tommy scored two goals at Highbury to knock Arsenal out of the FA Cup. Our son was just three weeks old at the time. I was very annoyed that Tommy came home so late after the match. I wanted to hear all about the game and I knew what time the train arrived and grew anxious, but of course the players had been celebrating in the nearest pub!

Tommy told the lads that he had better go and catch a bus home. Reg Foulkes told him that the last bus had gone long ago and ordered a taxi for him. When he arrived home he could hardly untie his shoelaces, but I later saw the funny side of it when I was presented with a gift of sausages, which he had received from a supporter.

He became unhappy at Norwich and signed for Newport County. We moved to Wales in 1954, when our son Neil was just nine months old.

The mountain goat of Newport

Once again, we shared a house in Llanthewy Road, this time with Ray Lawrence, who was Newport County's first-team trainer. It had a very steep hill. Pushing the pram up that huge hill, I must have looked like a mountain goat. Once again, there were no locks on any of the doors and we used the same entrance. That's where we stayed until we moved into a larger house just off Chepstow Road, which had been turned into four flats by the club. These had their own private entrances, and we had some space to ourselves at last.

Lawrence also had a long playing career as a centre-half with Gainsborough Trinity, Hull City and Newport, where he had a short spell as their caretaker-manager. He played at Swindon Town in the War League and at Haarlem, and he died in January 1987.

Annoyed with Leyton Orient

Life was alright in Newport, but my big complaint was that it rained more than in Manchester. Of course Tommy then moved to Leyton Orient in March 1956. We moved to 32 Durham Avenue in Woodford Green, Essex, but I was a little bit annoyed with the club because I was left to move house on my own, while Tommy was at the club. While I was pregnant with our daughter Alison, I got home help so that I could be with our son because I would not leave him with strangers after recently moving house.

Once again we were in a club house, with no telephone and a long way away from Oldham. All I can say is that you really do grow up quickly in this type of situation. I got another home help when Alison Jean Johnston was born in the morning of 6 December 1956. She was a big baby, weighing in at 10lb 4oz. To celebrate, Tommy scored four goals in three League matches.

Time to move again, off to Lancashire

As the seasons went by, Tommy was doing very well and having some great success with Leyton Orient. But the Happy Wanderer got it into his head it was time to move on again, and both Newcastle United and Sunderland had showed an interest in him, although they were both struggling in the First Division.

Tommy was keen on joining Blackburn Rovers, who were promotion contenders, with a great chance of getting into the First Division. He felt he was getting to a point where it was now or never; he didn't want to miss his chance of playing in a higher grade of football. I was very happy in Essex and wanted Tommy to stay with the O's, as I was quite content and settled.

In the end, we did go to Blackburn in March 1958, but I told Tommy very clearly not to make me his excuse. It would have been easy for him to say that he was leaving because his wife was homesick for the north, but after eight years away it would have been a complete lie. I did like living in Essex and made a nice friend and was very happy there.

Tommy unfortunately (or fortunately) did not like the Lancashire weather and he seemed to have a permanent cough. He helped Blackburn to promotion and was happy about that, but he wasn't really settled. In truth, he missed his friends at Leyton Orient and I missed living in Essex. He became unsettled and seemed to go to the pub more and more.

Back to Essex and Orient

Tommy returned to Leyton Orient in February 1959 and we went to stay at 275 Buckhurst Way in Buckhurst Hill in Essex, which was Dave Sexton's old Orient club house. Dave had gone to Crystal Palace. We settled in once again, and there was something different about Leyton Orient, compared with all the other clubs we had been with. The atmosphere was very good, the wives and children had their own little community and I was happy to be back in Essex. I made friends with Shirley Charlton, Stan's first wife. We were good friends, and went to the cinema together. Les and Amy Gore also lived in Buckhurst Way and we got along very well with them.

We were also friends with Bill and Helen Taylor. It was Tommy who got Billy to join Leyton Orient from Bonnyrigg Rose in Scotland but he didn't quite make it as a player. In later years he did achieve great things as a coach with England, before his sudden death.

Because Tommy didn't earn the type of wages footballers do now, we never had the money to buy our own house and always lived in a club-owned house. We paid £1 a week in rent. Tommy always supported people like Jimmy Hill who fought hard for the players to have decent contracts and for clubs to pay the players what they were worth.

My mother died in a place called Carlton, just outside Blackpool on 9 September 1961. It was quite a shock as she died very suddenly and we went back for the funeral.

Too old for Mr Carey, off to Kent

Tommy and the Orient boss Johnny Carey were not quite seeing eye-to-eye. Tom didn't want to look after the reserves on a reduced wage, which from my point of view was quite understandable.

I only learnt about Tommy's chat with Johnny Carey after he had left the club. I felt he should have gone to see Harry Zussman (the Leyton Orient chairman). I would have phoned Mr Zussman to find out about the reason for the drop in wages. After all Tommy had done for the club, I'm sure he would have overruled his manager.

Unfortunately, Tommy just accepted it because Carey was the manager – and to think, he was one of my favourite players when with Manchester United! Oh well, these things happen in life. Anyway, before I knew much about it, Tommy got an offer from Gillingham and we were on our travels again.

Gillingham, not my favourite

I got off on a very bad footing with Gillingham Football Club because when we got back from the funeral of my mother in Carlton, three men from Gillingham were waiting on our doorstep. Manager Harry Barratt, chairman Dr Grossmark, and trainer Bill Collins were all itching to get Tommy to sign for them. It was a difficult situation because my mother had just died and I didn't want to move. I wanted to stay in the comfort of my own home in Essex and close to my friends.

Anyway eventually I told Tommy to please himself and do what he wanted to do. He decided, no matter how sad it was, that it was the right time to move away from Brisbane Road, since he had little future as a first-team player under Mr Carey.

I must say, I was a little disgusted with these three gentlemen from Gillingham, being so insensitive and not allowing me time to grieve over my mother in private.

We moved into a house in Featherby Road, and we could see the River Medway when walking down to school to fetch the kids. We never settled even though we knew Gillingham's reserve half-back player Gordon Brown and his wife Joan. They soon moved back to her home town of Blackburn.

Tommy sickened by the bribes scandal, off to Folkestone

Things happened at Gillingham that sickened Tommy: four players accepted bribes to lose two games against Wrexham. The FA held an enquiry and the football club and the four players in question were cleared due to lack of evidence. Tommy decided he could not play for them again, so at the end of the season we were on the move again.

Tommy got a free transfer and we moved to Kent so that he could be player-coach of Folkestone Town in the Southern League. At the start of Tommy's second season with Folkestone he brought in the former Orient reserve goalkeeper Albert Cochran.

Albert and his wife Val became good friends and they were often our babysitters. Also there was Tony Biggs, whom we knew after his move from the Arsenal as part of the Len Julians deal when he joined Orient. He stayed a few days with us in our club house until he found his own digs in Essex because he lived in Middlesex.

We were much happier there than we had been in Gillingham, but Essex was a lovely place and I feel we should have stayed at Leyton Orient. Not many knew this, but Harry Zussman did offer Tommy a position for life at the club and I thought Tommy was rather silly to turn it down. On reflection, it was difficult to understand what that term 'job for life' actually meant.

Leaves football, opens a betting shop

Tommy called it a day in May 1964 and we moved to Poulton-Le-Fylde, just outside Blackpool, during the following November. We opened a betting office and it was very strange for me because I had to learn all about the betting game. Tommy knew all about betting shops, but I learned everything from a lovely old gentleman who did the boards named Mr Allender. Tommy just accepted I would learn all about the betting game; he was not a teacher and never had the patience to teach me.

I actually wanted Tommy to open a sports shop and cash in on his name, but he didn't think opening one in the north would work. I could never understand how Tommy could be so positive on the field, yet so negative off it.

We were hit financially by the betting tax and I said to Tommy, 'If the betting tax went up again, we would have to sell the shop'. Tommy wondered how we would manage. However, we decided to emigrate to Australia because we felt there was more opportunity for our children.

We arrive in Australia

Before we decided on Australia, I sent off for some literature from South Africa House and New Zealand House. Finally, we decided on Oz. After being here a few years and seeing the goings-on in Soweto, South Africa, my son said to me, 'It's good we didn't go to South Africa, you would have been thrown in jail!'.

We closed the betting shop about 12 months prior to going to Australia. After packing our belongings to ship to Oz I got a job in a supermarket and Tommy worked as a labourer with a couple of friends on a building site.

I think it was a great move. My eldest sister was already in Australia and kindly said that she and her husband would be our sponsors. Dinah and Bill Bradley had arrived in Australia in October 1969. They were pig farmers and they paid their own fares after receiving compensation for loss of livelihood from the Wilson government for the compulsory purchase of their pig farm in the UK.

They sponsored us and when we arrived we went to live on their 129-acre farm in a small town named Dapto. Dapto was between 8 and 10km from Wollongong in New South Wales, a beautiful seaside resort with a number of steelworks in an industrial area.

I don't think Tommy would have lasted the pace if we had had to move into one of those migrant hostels. He went down to the local club and it was like walking into a local pub at home… it was full of English, Scots, Irish and even a Welshman. This helped Tommy settle in quicker than anything else. Tommy would go to play snooker at the Dapto Leagues club and he soon made new friendships. Over the years he won a number of minor trophies for darts and snooker and played for many years in the local Illawarra League.

In 1974 Dave Sexton brought his Chelsea side on tour to Australia and we met and had dinner together; it was a very enjoyable evening. He came to the Orb Bowling Club – owned by Lysaghts, whose works team Tommy coached. Later in the week, we visited him and his Chelsea team in the Wollongong Hotel.

A personal note

When I first met Tommy I didn't actually know what had happened to his left arm, although I knew he had a problem. While on a visit to his family in Loanhead in June 1952 I learned about his mining accident. He showed me his wrist for the first time. I really feel that this was one of the reasons he was so shy – it was not only because he was a dour Scot.

I always thought that when a young man danced with a young lady, he would have her right hand in his left hand. Tommy never did this. I always told Tommy that he should think himself lucky that he didn't lose his arm completely. Having hurt his wrist at that young age, his left arm did not develop as with his right arm and he was very self-conscious about it.

I think after the accident the family spoiled him because he spent over two years in and out of hospital because of this terrible accident. He got quite used to having his own way.

He always did wear a bandage and was absolutely horrified when he got to Norwich City that they wore short sleeved shirts. I didn't see the problem but he turned around and asked me 'What do I do?' and I replied 'You get out and play'. He came home one night and told me 'They keep asking me why I wear a bandage.' I said 'Fine, tell them what happened, and then they will stop asking'.

This was the very first time he had actually told anyone. Up to this point he had always worn the bandage at home as well – after all, it had been quite a serious accident – but he stopped after the Norwich discussion. His mother once said 'Our Tommy isn't wearing his bandage'. I replied 'Yes, he doesn't need to anymore'. On the football field, though, he felt safer with his bandage on.

I remember Tommy's big day for Norwich City, scoring the two goals that knocked Arsenal out of the FA Cup. I was busy looking after our three-week-old baby Neil. We had no television in those days and it was a neighbour who told me the score. I would have loved to have seen a news reel of those goals and the celebrations.

I must say, like most couples, Tommy and I had our arguments, but we certainly connected on the game of football. Tommy took after his family members, brought up in those days in a small mining village. The man was the head of the household and mother stayed home and worked in the house and looked after the kids. The menfolk in those days would work hard down the mines, they came home and played hard, and by that I mean they liked to bet, they liked their pint and they liked their football and in that way, it was all outgoing energy.

Tommy then met me, a very outgoing Lancashire lass, and my father had made me aware of my rights and taught me not to back down for anyone. I was brought up in a totally different way to Tommy. We were allowed to express ourselves, but one thing was the same: you did get a clip round the ear if you did something wrong.

This book is the very first time that Tommy has really spoken about his boyhood. I always said that if Tommy had my personality to go with his talent, he would have been a world-beater in football, no doubt about it. But when we had arguments I was quite stubborn and

I wouldn't be the little housewife Tommy wanted me to be. It was not in my makeup at all to be told that he was the head of the house.

We had two lovely children and my life settled into a pattern when our son Neil was born. I enjoyed having my little friend, as when Tommy was away playing, it could be very lonely. But now I had this boy to care for and as he started to grow up Neil and I had great conversations and he spoke very clearly.

Unhappy with the Scottish selectors

Tommy was unhappy with the way things were going and being continually overlooked by the Scottish selector. Many a time I felt hurt for him because he should have played for Scotland, there was no doubt about that. He really was the best centre-forward in the UK between 1957 and 1959 but there was lot of snobbishness within the Scottish Football Association.

They always seem to look to the English First Division and players from the Scottish League. They just would not go down to the levels of a little club like Leyton Orient; andyet Tommy was the leading goalscorer in the whole country at the time, outscoring everyone, including Brian Clough and Jackie Mudie. That told me, and many others at the time, that he should have been capped.

There was a lot of politics at the Scottish FA and I really felt sorry for Tommy. I bet if he were an Englishman, he would have played for his country.

A wonderful man, Mr Les Gore

Tommy took being overlooked by Scotland pretty hard, but Les Gore was really a great friend and an exceptional man and team manager. It was funny that he never wanted to be called manager, yet he did a great job for Leyton Orient Football Club, and had a way with the players. He was a gentleman in the truest meaning of the word and he had a lot of patience with Tommy, who could be quite temperamental. Les also came from the working classes. He always was one of the lads and he knew how to handle and get the best out of Tommy and the other lads.

We were both very upset when we heard of the death of Les Gore back in January 1991. Before his death, we received a letter from him in which he remarked how the transfer fees of players were going crazy. He wrote, 'If Tommy Johnston was playing now, would he have been the first million-pound player transfer? Yes, Tommy Johnston was an excellent centre-forward'.

> *Coventry-born Frederick Leslie Gore was a real Leyton Orient man, having served the club as player, trainer, coach and acting manager and manager between 1951 and 1966. Les died on 22 January 1991, a day before his 77th birthday. In* The Men Who Made Leyton Orient FC *by authors Neilson Kaufman and Alan Ravenhill, it says at the end of Les's profile: 'Gore should hold a prominent place in the history of Leyton Orient Football Club' and correctly so. We'll miss you Les.*

The other problem Tommy had is that he moved around the clubs very quickly during the early part of his career. I truly believe with all my heart that if Tommy and I had not got married, he would not have stayed with Norwich City, Newport County or with Leyton Orient for very long. He hated being in lodgings all on his own. The fact that he was in someone else's house, and couldn't say or eat what he wanted, or do anything as he liked, used to upset him. He was, and still is to a certain extent, quite a shy man. If he weren't married, he would have had to stay in lodgings and not a club house like we had in Norwich and Essex, and I don't think he would have stayed with any of the clubs for very long.

I remember talking one day in Loanhead to Tommy's brother Alex's wife Bunty about Tommy's life and career and she paid me a compliment. She said to me, 'Jean, you made Tommy Johnston'. I know Tommy doesn't think like that but in some ways it was true.

It wasn't the fact that it was me, but by just being a married man at the time, he got his own home and could settle, and I think this was the real start of Tommy Johnston becoming the great player that he was. Although we still moved around – my mother once remarked we were like a pair of gypsies and should be living in a caravan – the stability of the family helped him play better.

I became a great packer and within 11 months we went from Essex to Blackburn and back to Essex again. I think that if Tommy hadn't married he would have drifted even more from club to club and maybe not achieved as he did. We had to take everything with us when we moved because we didn't have the money to buy new furnishings. We had to 'make fit' with whatever we could in the way of curtains and so on as we were always in a club house.

I did love meeting all the new people, but it annoyed me that the likes of Tommy, Jimmy Hill and many others of the day had to fight very hard to negotiate player contracts. I think the wages that the top players are getting today are absolutely ludicrous, but players like Tommy were worth a little bit more than they actually got.

It was an interesting life as a footballer's wife. We did hit a few dark spots, and if Tommy wasn't happy, as previously mentioned, he would go to the pub a little bit more than he should have done. However, there were also plenty of times when we had the most wonderful times together, like when Leyton Orient took all the players and their wives and children on holiday to the Channel Islands in May 1961 for 10 days. There were over 40 of us. The boys won their three matches, beating Beeches Association 2–0, Guernsey Amalgamated 6–0 (Tommy hit three goals) and a League of Jersey Select side 3–1. It was more of a fun thing for the players and Tommy enjoyed playing in the matches, although all the squad got a run-out.

We virtually took over the hotel and we all had a glorious time. I remember after one of the matches seeing them all troop back into the hotel with their kit on – they had to clean up there. We formed a bit of a group on the holiday, with Phil White and his wife and son, George Wright and his wife and son, and the four of us. We hired a car between us for the 10 days but only George could drive and we had the four adults and six kids in the car for trips to the beach, but after a few days word reached us from the authorities that we should stop overcrowding the car. It was left to poor old George Wright to act as our chauffeur, going backwards and forwards every day.

I remember the hotel had a large fishpond in the rear garden and some of the lads took bets on whose children would fall in first. The favourites were Stan Charlton's kids. In the end, it was Frank George's young fellow, with all his clothes on – drinks all round, Mr George!

It was a fun time in the Channel Islands, the weather was good, the lads played golf and enjoyed the motorised go-carts and the wives enjoyed the sun. Such trips were made possible and all paid for by Harry Zussman and Leslie Grade, two wonderful gentlemen who not only cared about the club but also about the players and their families.

Leslie, and to a lesser extent his brothers Lew Grade and Bernard Delfont, were all involved with the O's. They often got the Orient lads complimentary tickets for shows in the West End. The highlight for me was going to the Royal Command Performance on 16 May 1960; I still have the programme. My favourite singer Nat King Cole was on the bill and it was the first time we saw Sammy Davis Jr live. It was a great show.

Tommy had a very special friendship with Monty Berman, but unfortunately I never had the pleasure of meeting him. Having been in amateur theatricals myself it would have given me a lot of pleasure rummaging around his offices.

Tommy the prankster

A 'house devil' and a 'street angel' is what you would call Tommy: if someone outside the house says they want something done, Tommy goes out of his way to run and help, but at home – well, no comment. But he's still quite a popular man, quite a prankster. Tommy couldn't pass a joke shop anywhere without going in and buying something.

He was christened Tommy Cooper by a friend of mine and at parties he would open up completely after a couple of beers. He would tell stories by the dozen and the young ones loved the magic of the scarves changing colour and the many card tricks he performed.

Tommy still has one trick he bought in Glasgow in 1949, before I knew him. It's a Dracula's Coffin, with a slot on the top, and you put a 10-cent piece on the top and a hand shoots out and it takes all the money inside the coffin. This fascinated the children and they would ask their parents for more and more 10 cents so they could watch Dracula steal the money. However, the mothers and fathers soon cottoned on! In the end, when Tommy looked inside the coffin the money had disappeared – it even baffled him. I asked my children, Neil and Alison, if they had taken the money and Alison said 'I did'. I asked her why and she said, 'Well I needed the money'. There was really no answer to that!

Tommy loves children until they start answering back. He says they are cheeky, and I say 'No, they're just children'.

More patriotic as he grows older

As Tommy has got older, I think he has become more patriotic. He is still very much Scottish. If they had the weather, he would love to be transported back to Loanhead. He would be quite at home and he could drift back into that lifestyle, but I couldn't.

He follows the same pattern in his life now. He goes down for a drink on a Monday and a Wednesday to chat with his friend. He still likes his little bet on the horses. He doesn't smoke anymore, he gave that up a few years back. He will never change because that is his lifestyle. I'm quite happy living in my adopted country of Oz, very happy in fact, and I've made some wonderful friends here. I worked in the K-Mart from 1974 until I retired 14 years later.

There's an old saying that whatever you learn in life is never wasted or forgotten and its true. When I was at K-Mart, I modelled the clothes when the new spring and summer fashions arrived. I was the Union official at K-Mart for 14 years. I loved it there and they were like family to me.

Christened 'Grumpy'

As you know, Tommy was very fondly thought of in his football days. At Lysaghts I was his general dogsbody – I ran the canteen and sold raffle tickets. I remember his first payment for running the

Lysaghts football team was a second-hand garden hose and a lawnmower, but they were very welcome I might add, as we were very strapped for cash having just moved into our first home in Dapto.

Some of the players christened him 'Grumpy' and over the years it stuck, but Tommy didn't take offence. So I believe it has been quite good for us in Australia and wherever we have gone we have made friends.

I don't know what it is with the Scottish people, they weren't allowed to show any emotions or a soft side and I think Billy Connolly has touched on that very well. I know Tommy thinks the world of his grandsons but he can't actually give them a hug, which is sad because he can't show affection. I make sure that they give him a hug when they first walk through the door. Men must show their feelings and not take females for granted.

One of the things Tommy has omitted to mention was how important his brothers were to him. Harry died in 1991, but Tommy was always the closest to Jimmy. They were, and still are, the best of pals, and they still write regularly. Jimmy was virtually waiting on young Tom and his wife Isobel's doorstep after they picked us up at Edinburgh Airport when we stayed with them when we were there on holiday in 1989. We have never been able to get Jimmy on a plane, but Tommy would have loved Jimmy to come over on holiday – they are very much alike in temperament.

Tommy diagnosed with bowel cancer
During September 1991 Tommy and I discovered he had bowel cancer. He had an operation the following November. Tommy actually delayed the surgery so that he could present the prizes for his local snooker club, to the horror of the family. He lost about 18 inches of the bowel and has a permanent colostomy pouch or bag, as they sometimes call it.

It was a rough time for Tommy and the family and he lost over 10 kilos in a couple of weeks as he couldn't eat anything. But like most things in life you learn to overcome these setbacks.

Unfortunately, the location of the pouch was on the skin where the skin graft was done in 1945 after the mining accident, so it was already weakened.

Tommy managed well for a number of years and he even managed to play a little game of golf and lawn bowls. After over eight years, he started to have trouble again and he had a prolapse, which started to get worse and worse. In January 2000 he had to go for further surgery to have the prolapse refashioned. A mesh insert was placed inside to strengthen the area and correct the problem.

The surgeon insisted that both the golf and lawn bowls had to go, along with heavy lifting, so nowadays Tommy is very limited in what he can do. This did cause enormous problems for Tommy because he had always been a physical person, involved in playing golf and snooker. More recently he had sciatica in his hip, which isn't very good either, and he really misses his sport. Nowadays he reads sports books and magazines but he won't actually pick up a novel.

He enjoys watching sport and the football on television and reading books and articles on Leyton Orient. He loves the sports programmes on television and watches nearly every soccer match – they often start at around 6.30am – and he also enjoys watching videos.

Tommy's 70th birthday

Tommy had a wonderful and great surprise arrive on his 70th birthday on 18 August 1997. It was another tankard sent by Martin P. Smith from the Leyton Orient International Supporters' Club for his birthday, and it got quite a lot of attention in the local press. Tommy was so happy that he was still remembered by the supporters of Orient. These were the best presents he has ever received. Now he has the three tankards, two from Orient and one from Folkestone. They all take pride of place in our lounge for everyone to see and Tommy looks at them all every morning.

A word about our children

I don't think Tommy realised what effect his career had on the children. Going from town to town they had to settle in at different schools very quickly and make new friends, and it wasn't easy for them.

Our son Neil had his 18th birthday up in the sky in a jet going over to Australia. The captain actually wished him a happy birthday, with a little prompting from me. Neil had been at grammar school in the UK and got nine O-level passes and was heading for university. But when we arrived in Australia we were told that Neil would have to go back to High School for a final year to sit his entrance exams. Tommy was furious about this but I told him to just play the game and go along with it.

Neil did well in catching up and won the John Lysaghts maths prize. He passed his exams and went to Wollongong University where he became a civil engineer.

Our daughter Alison decided she would rather join the workforce. She had brains, and she could have gone to university. I didn't approve of her leaving school but she was a determined girl. However, she later returned to her studies and became very competent, later going to college to do other courses.

Alison and her husband, Kevin Bull, now live near us in Sanctuary Point. They have a little girl named Rebecca Mae, who is 11 years old, and twin boys, Colin Thomas and Philip Craig, who have just turned nine. They are really delightful, we have them here on a regular basis, but I must admit that these days it is nice for Tommy to have just one of the boys at a time.

Like all good men Tommy spoilt his little girl, and he still does today, even though she is a very 'grown-up married woman'.

Our son Neil and his wife Suzanne (Suzie) live in Brisbane with their daughters Liesie and Amy. It's quite a distance from Sanctuary Point to Brisbane and Tommy has got it into his head that he has finished with travelling after all these years. We miss seeing our son Neil regularly but work has taken him to Brisbane and there is nothing we can do about that. At least we have our daughter Alison and her family close to us.

My final word

One of the things this book has done is to get Tommy to talk about his childhood, growing up in Loanhead, his mine accident and his football memories in such great detail.

Tommy has always been down to earth – he loved the accolades, but who wouldn't. He loved the game, but he was a working man and all his stardom never ever affected him. Yes, Tommy Johnston was a great centre-forward, but don't tell him I said so!

His family in Scotland were and are still very proud of Tommy's achievements in the game of football after all his early setbacks as a young boy.

Now, in 2004, we are still happily living on the coast at 156 Links Avenue, Sanctuary Point, New South Wales (NSW), Australia. We had our house built between 1988 and 1989, moving in two weeks before Easter 1989. It's about 200 yards up the Avenue from the St George's Basin Country Club, ideal for Tommy to have his social drink twice a week.

I hope my few words will have given an insight into Tommy, the man and the top-class footballer, and our life together. I have some wonderful words framed. They say: 'God grant me the serenity to accept the things I cannot change, courage to change the things I can and wisdom to know the difference'. It's the last sentence that sometimes has me beaten!

A few memories from Alison Jean Bull (née Johnston)

I'm sorry to say I don't have many memories of my Dad's playing days. My major claim to fame is that I was born in 1956, the year that Dad won promotion to the Second Division with Leyton Orient, so obviously my being born must have inspired him to even greater things. I believe over the next few seasons he was just unstoppable. A daughter's influence!

My first real memory of him playing football was with Folkestone Town, but then we soon moved in 1964 to Poulton-Le-Fylde, near Blackpool, so it looks like I missed all the best periods of Dad's career. I'm told that I first attended school at Woodford Green

Infants in Essex. I remember going to school in Folkestone when I was about six years old and I was eight and a half when we moved to Poulton. Mum and Dad first applied to come to Oz when I was about 11. I was quite excited about it but things began to drag on a bit and by the time we actually did emigrate, I was already 15 and into puberty and all that. I was about to lose all my best friends and in all honesty, I wouldn't have been very disappointed if we had never left England because it was hard to leave my friends.

I eventually got into the swing of things in Oz with our new home and new school. A few years later I enjoyed playing football and became a good athlete, so the family had another star player in its ranks! Neil was also a good player. It was in the Johnston blood.

In 1979 I played for a football team called the Bulli Thunderbirds and, as one article states, the Bullis had a 'Heart of Goals'. We scored 69 goals without reply, which helped us reach the NSW Champion of Champions competition. After that I continued with my studies and went into the workplace, so football had to stop, and I was getting too old for it anyway.

I went back to England on holiday in 1980. One of my first visits was to Brisbane Road to watch an Orient game and see for myself the place where Dad broke all his records. They beat Wrexham 4–0, on a cold and rainy February day. I met a lot of people who still remembered Dad after more than 20 years and also I had some photos taken with Sid Bishop, a former colleague of Dad's.

It was during this trip that I first realised how beautiful Australia is and I certainly became more appreciative of the lifestyle that we have here. I got married to Kevin Bull, have three wonderful kids, and the rest, as they say, is history.

A few memories from Neil Thomas Johnston

I do not have many memories of my Dad during the early part of his career with Leyton Orient, although I remember when he joined Blackburn Rovers in March 1958. Even though I was a youngster at the time, I can remember the feeling that Blackburn was a much bigger club than Leyton Orient. The stadium and the crowd seemed much larger to me, as well as the noise of the fans.

When Dad returned to Leyton Orient in 1959, I can recall going to the ground on a few occasions, usually when Dad was having treatment. My sister Alison and I often went to matches with Mum. I can recall there was a tea room where we used to go at half-time for a drink and a bit of a warm-up.

One memory I have is of the O's FA Cup run in the 1960–61 season, a third-round tie at the Priestfield Stadium in Gillingham that we won 6–2 – Dad scored the opener and made a few others. I then went with friends of Mum and Dad's, John Short and his wife Beryl, to see Orient in action in the fourth round of the Cup at the Dell against Southampton, which O's surprisingly won 1–0. I do recall it being very wet. We got there very early and I loved watching the Fire Brigade removing water from the playing surface.

The fifth-round cup match was a glamour tie for Orient against Sheffield Wednesday, with 31,000 people crammed into Brisbane Road. Wednesday had some good international players including goalkeeper Ron Springett. We lost 0–2, but we had our chances to score first.

At the end of the game, when everyone had left the ground, we went to look at the television cameras on the floodlight pylon. Yes, Dad and Leyton Orient were on television. Alison and I wandered over that way and there were large amounts of film with all the action from the game, frame by frame, strewn all over the floor. I wish we had been good little kids and cleaned it all up and taken it home – I'm sure there would have been some nice action shots of Dad.

Move to Gillingham

The move to Gillingham was a real shock to me. We had belted the daylights out of them in the FA Cup the previous season and I wondered why on earth my Dad would go there. I was too young to understand that footballers, like people, do age and they don't last at the highest level forever. It was a sad time in our lives. I don't think anyone really wanted to leave Leyton Orient. I subsequently found out that Dad and the new Orient boss Johnny Carey did not see eye-to-eye, even though he had taken Dad from Orient to Blackburn Rovers and, from what I have read in later years, it was Dad who helped Rovers to promotion.

I heard that the relationship between them deteriorated (or perhaps it never developed). So when Carey came to Orient, Dad got dumped in the reserves and that meant a pay-cut, so he decided to move on. I could never understand Carey. My Dad was good enough to get Blackburn into the old First Division, but just two years later he was not good enough to play for him in the Second Division? It didn't make sense. All of us were sad to leave and the Orient supporters were sad to see Dad go.

The only game I can really remember at Gillingham is Dad's debut versus Millwall. I sat in the main stand, in the same area that we had sat in the season before when Orient won the cup-tie. The stand was fairly full – there were over 8,000 in the stadium – and I could feel a sense of expectation around the place. Dad scored on his debut, with a header of course, and it was their first win of the season after nine straight League and Cup defeats. Gillingham won the match 3–1.

However, this was probably the lowest time that I can recall. Not all went well, particularly when the match-fixing scandal broke. As far as I knew Dad was one of the people that brought the ugly business out into the light of day. It was not nice seeing Priestfield Stadium on the news for all the wrong reasons during April 1962; and so during May we left Gillingham.

I do recall that Dad was involved in a nasty car accident just after signing for Folkestone Town and he was out for some time due to his injuries. I remember Dad started his return to full fitness by doing some training on his own, and on a couple of occasions I joined him. It was the first time I had some 'real' football training – at nine years old.

Folkestone turned out to be a very pleasant experience for us all. Not just the place itself, but the whole atmosphere, which had improved no end. My parents met some nice people at the football club, who were all very friendly – just like at Leyton Orient.

Dad was player-coach and Folkestone were in the Southern League Division One. I think Dad's first season in his new role was a real learning experience. Then he brought in a few more experienced players, including Albert Cochran, a fine goalkeeper signed from Leyton Orient. The second season of Dad's stay in the 1963–64 season was also a good one. A home programme from January 1964 indicates that Dad was the top goalscorer for Folkestone in Southern League matches on four goals – in half a season! He didn't appear in the team a lot during his second season with them.

I ferreted out some of the Folkestone Town programmes of the time and found a few interesting facts. In the 1962–63 season, when Dad joined them, Folkestone were in the Southern League Division One and the reserves played in the Seanglian League. The following season they were in the same League and won promotion to the Southern League Premier Division.

Non-League football had its attractions for me, as I was able to wander around the ground with freedom. The very best memory I have of that season was when Dad, at that time 37 years old, took me to watch him on my 10th birthday on 4 January 1964. He was in the first team for a rare appearance at Deal Town. They won 3–1 and Dad gave me a nice extra birthday present by scoring a hat-trick.

During Dad's last season, 1963–64, Folkestone Town won promotion back to the Southern League Premier Division, winning 28 of the 42 games played and picking up 63 points. They beat Kings Lynn to the championship by just two points, with Corby Town finishing in a close third position. We then left Folkestone and moved north to Poulton-Le-Fylde, where Dad started as a bookmaker.

Move to Australia

When we first came to Australia in January 1972, I had my birthday on the plane. I remember it was a rush: we had only heard from Australia House on 17 December 1971, Mum's birthday, about the travel arrangements. We had all of 16 days to sort ourselves out, say cheerio to families and get to London for the flight, and it was all over Christmas and New Year.

Dad became the coach of the Lysaghts soccer team a month or so later. I had turned 18 and had already played senior football for a couple of years in an amateur League in Blackpool prior to emigrating. Generally I had been a goalkeeper in school football, but I had also played a few games in a left-midfield role. One look at the hard Aussie grounds convinced me that my days as a goalie were over. Not quite, as it turned out.

Lysaghts, a steel company originally from Bristol, England, provided good sports facilities with a cricket oval and a football pitch, squash, tennis and a bowling club at Figtree. I can recall an interstate cricket match between New South Wales and South Australia being played on the ground.

Dad's first training session was a real eye-opener. There were just a few of us: the club president, who came to watch, and his son, Dad and me, Stevie Lawler and a short Italian migrant named Abe Calveresi. It was a month before our first game and here we were, just four of us – one Italian, two 18-year-olds and Dad. Our first year was a struggle to say the least but at least we had fun.

There is one thing I can mention that probably none of the others can – and that is about Dad as a coach. When I joined the ranks of senior football, I had ideas about what to expect – lots of training, much harder than when I was a schoolboy player, and inspirational and motivating team-talks from the coach before you went on the field.

This did not happen with Dad. His theory was that a footballer would do a lot more running and do it willingly, if he had a football to chase instead of mindless running round an athletic track. So training sessions tendered to involve a lot of games and shooting practice and how to take corners, free-kicks and so on.

The next notable thing was the lack of a big team-talk. I don't think Dad felt comfortable as a public speaker, so we didn't do it. He would just come onto the field and have a chat to individuals or sometimes talk to two or three players that had to work together. The personal touch seemed to get better results.

Well, the word soon got around about the new coaching methods of Tommy Johnston and more players turned up for coaching the following season, including some far better-quality players. We developed into a couple of fair teams.

Sometimes in later years, when we were short of players, Dad would have a run out. One match clearly stands out in my mind. He had to put on the boots at the age of 46. He didn't run around much, just got the ball and laid it off, but when we got a corner, oh boy!

There was a promising 18-year-old centre-half in the other team who Dad wanted to sign. Well, Dad beat him repeatedly in the air, scoring one goal where I swear that Dad's shoulder was above this lad's head.

I had a great view, standing at the back post, and it really amazed me. I thought that for someone who hadn't played for maybe seven or eight years, it was just incredible how high he could still jump, literally inches above everyone else.

Another thing was the Johnston 'double act' in reserve grade. In the space of five games, Lysaghts scored something like 15 goals – of which Dad and I got 11 between us. Even though Dad was not as mobile on the field, all you had to do was put the ball in the right place and he could beat opponents 20 years his junior.

Lysaghts had a couple of average years and invited Dad back as coach. In this second spell as coach, which lasted four years, he took both the first team and reserves to the final play-offs and then the reserves to the Grand Final.

After I completed my studies, I moved to Sydney to start my career as an engineer – and I still have a love of the game of soccer. Since I finished playing, nothing else has really taken its place as far as sporting activities go.

My final thought is just to say that my Dad must have really been something in his prime.

Section Two: The authors on Tommy

In researching this book the authors uncovered a large body of evidence that proves beyond doubt just how good the big Scottish forward really was.

The reporters of the day regularly praised Johnston in their accounts of the matches he played in, and many of their comments are reproduced in this section. In addition, countless fans wrote letters to him over the years expressing their appreciation of his skills, and many of these are quoted in the pages that follow.

Tommy's special qualities, that really make him stand out as a player, are looked at by the authors in detail in this part of the book. His heading ability was his greatest asset, but by no means the whole story: Tommy could score goals with his feet too, and was an expert reader of the game as well as a strong influence on the rest of the side.

A look at the list of the all-time top scorers in the English League serves to put Tommy's achievements in their proper context: he deserves his place among the most prolific scorers that the game has seen to date.

Chapter 12

What the press said

The authors of this book have collected many newspaper articles on the O's since 1936 and have consulted every match report featuring Tommy Johnston. His goals were described by the various writers, who used many different descriptions in describing his play: wonderful, beautiful, glorious, great, fine, classy, magnificent, lovely, powerful, characteristic, superb, amazing, perfect, clever, excellent, sizzling, scorching, delightful, neat, spectacular, delicate. All these words emphasise just how good his play was.

There were a number of top-quality football writers of Johnston's era who appeared to really appreciate his true ability, in particular John Morgan, Bob Pennington and Norman Dixon. They were not concerned that Johnston wasn't playing for Arsenal, Tottenham Hotspur or Manchester United; they saw him for what he was – a damn good player. The fact that he played for Leyton Orient at the time made no difference to them.

John Morgan often wrote about Tommy's top-class ability and he did not allow any prejudice about lower division clubs to cloud his judgement. Bob Pennington often wrote that Johnston should be selected for Scotland. Unlike the selectors of the day he was not narrow-minded, but unfortunately his good sense did not prevail with the Scottish decision-makers. Norman Dixon was also a very good sports reporter who did not resort to saying things that everyone expected him to say. He always wrote what he thought and would give lesser-known players the praise they deserved when other reporters seemed to pass over them. In this way, Dixon often praised the likes of Tommy Johnston.

The craggy Scot

Tommy Johnston was often described in match reports and articles as a 'craggy Scot'. Craggy is not a derogatory description. It suggests a rugged type of looks: Stan Charlton and Ted Phillips spring to mind as other examples. So 'craggy' was a reasonable word to use to describe Tommy. Orient certainly had some more elegant-looking players over the years, like Jimmy Blair and Glenn Roeder. Tommy Johnston and Stan Charlton were the opposite in looks, although all four men were superb players.

Tommy's wife Jean feels that the description of Tommy as a craggy Scot sums up his personality as well as his looks. She regards players like him as determined and consistent – not giving an inch and expecting no favours – always out to win. Tommy was also often referred to as a dour Scot, which was quite true. It was rare to see him smiling in pictures or celebrating a goal. Tommy just shook hands with his colleagues, then ran back to the centre circle to get on with the match.

Extracts from match reports and articles on Tommy Johnston

These quotes have come from different articles by many football reporters. It may seem from the glowing praise that follows that the authors have left out the not-so-flattering reports. But the fact is there simply aren't any. Reading through the material it becomes clear just how high a standard of performance Tommy maintained throughout his career.

The newspapers that these extracts were taken from include: *Daily Mirror, Daily Herald, Daily Express, News Chronicle, Daily Mail, News of the World, Sunday Pictorial, The People, Empire News, Reynolds News, Lincolnshire Echo, Bristol Evening Post, Liverpool*

Echo, Walthamstow Guardian, Walthamstow Post, Stratford Express, Daily Telegraph, Sunday Telegraph, Sunday Express, Hackney Gazette, The Observer and even *The New York Times.*

His days with Norwich City

'Shrewsbury had no answer to the impressive Norwich City attack, in which 4-goal Tommy Johnston was easily their star-man.'
Shrewsbury Town 1 Norwich City 8 (Division Three South), 13 September 1952

Mighty Arsenal knocked out of the Cup by Tommy Johnston

'It was a memorable day after for the Norwich City supporters and players alike, especially the big blonde forward Tommy Johnston who scored both the Canaries' goals with glorious headers.'

'Hail the hero of Highbury! The man who knocked the mighty Arsenal out of the FA Cup was Norwich City's ex-Loanhead miner Tommy Johnston who cracked home two wonderful headed goals. Ironically, he only played because of an injury to Johnny Summers, the craggy Scot was so unhappy at being always left out of the side, he asked for a transfer. I wonder if City will sell now. The Arsenal fans were asking who is this Norwich power-house reserve centre-forward named Johnston. He is better and more skilful than many of the First Division forwards seen at Highbury this season.' *From a Scottish newspaper*

'Scotsman Tommy Johnston, a reserve player with Third Division South side Norwich City headed two wonder goals which knocked the reigning League champions Arsenal out of the FA Cup fourth round.' *The New York Times*
Arsenal 1 Norwich City 2 (FA Cup, fourth round), 30 January 1954

Danger men

'B-E-W-A-R-E- these eight men are the most dangerous in football. Stanley Matthews of Stoke City's magical feet, Tom Finney, Preston's power-man, Eddie Bailey, Spurs trickster, Ray Barlow, West Brom's link-man, Jackie Sewell, Sheffield Wednesday's prompter, Jackie Froggatt, Portsmouth's live-wire, Dennis Pacey's Leyton Orient express and Tommy Johnston, Norwich's ace menace No 1.'

Authors' Note: It is also nice to see O's youngster Dennis Pacey in this group, along with another who later appeared for the O's, Eddie Baily.

Tommy's days with Newport County

'Three times Tommy Johnston gave watchful Stan Aldous the slip to find the net, he was mobbed by many excited home spectators after the match.'

Newport County 3 Leyton Orient 0 (Division Three South), 5 October 1955

Authors' Note: Unfortunately, according to the Newport County historian Anthony Ambrosen, all the press articles and match reports in the local Newport Library on Newport County have been cut out.

Johnston's time at Leyton Orient

'Tommy Johnston on his Orient debut was responsible for giving Orient two goals in the first 20 minutes, he pushed a short pass to Phil Woosnam to score in the 10th minute and then on 20 minutes Johnston himself headed a beautiful goal.'

Swindon Town 1 Leyton Orient 2 (Division Three South), 25 February 1956

'Tommy Johnston kept Orient's front line moving sweetly and was particularly dangerous with his Tommy Lawton look-alike headers.'

Leyton Orient 8 Aldershot 3 (Division Three South), 17 March 1956

'On this display, Tommy Johnston is the best centre-forward in the Third Division.'

Crystal Palace 1 Leyton Orient 2 (Division Three South), 24 March 1956

'In the centre, Tommy Johnston fitted in perfectly. His craggy

features may make him look more than his 28 years, but his quick intelligent play suggests he could give Second Division centre-halves plenty to think about next season.'
Leyton Orient 5 Shrewsbury Town 2 (Division Three South), 14 April 1956

Johnston's goal puts Orient into Division Two

'Orient battled and sweated back into Division Two for the first time since 1929 with two points over Millwall before 22,337 fans. Nineteen minutes from time, the untiring Tommy Johnston, whose transfer from Newport has proved to be a masterstroke as he sent hats into the air by the O's fans, scored what proved to be the winning shot. The goal was fittingly made by the O's captain, 32-year-old Stan Aldous, who has played a great part in Orient's triumphant season.'
Leyton Orient 2 Millwall 1 (Division Three South), 26 April 1956

'As always, centre-forward Johnston was the star of the Leyton attack.'
Grimsby Town 0 Leyton Orient 0 (Division Two), 8 September 1956

'At centre-forward, Orient has in Johnston a truly fine player.'
Leyton Orient 3 Swansea Town 0 (Division Two), 20 October 1956

'Johnston clinched a win for Orient in the 80th minute. His header went in like a rocket and Harry Hough in goal hadn't a chance.'
Leyton Orient 2 Barnsley 0 (Division Two), 3 November 1956

'Johnston reduced the arrears with a cracking header from a perfectly placed Phil White cross.'
Sheffield United 2 Leyton Orient 3 (Division Two), 27 October 1956

'In the 63rd minute, Ronnie Heckman sent a perfect cross to Johnston's head. The ball was smashed into the back of the net before goalkeeper John Quairney could even move.'

Leyton Orient 2 Rotherham United 1 (Division Two), 17 November 1956

'Tommy Johnston troubled Lincoln centre-half Tony Emery more often than most centre-forwards do – he led Orient's attack with skill.'
Lincoln City 0 Leyton Orient 2 (Division Two), 24 November 1956

'Big Tommy Johnston saved Orient's table climbing from a surprise ending with a great equaliser 90 seconds from time in this fantastic thriller. Brisbane Road erupted. It might have been a Cup final goal.'
Leyton Orient 2 Bristol City 2 (Division Two), 1 December 1956

'After 19 minutes, Tommy Johnston headed a picture perfect goal from a Jimmy Smith centre.'
Fulham 3 Leyton Orient 1 (Division Two), 8 December 1956

'Johnston burst through from his own half to score a great second goal for Orient.'
Nottingham Forest 1 Leyton Orient 2 (Division Two), 15 December 1956

'Johnston persistently worried the Bury defence with great skill.'
Bury 1 Leyton Orient 3 (Division Two), 29 December 1956

'Chelsea's defence was rather lucky to survive without conceding a goal. Orient's lively attack caused all sorts of problems, particularly Johnston and Phil White.'
Leyton Orient 0 Chelsea 2 (FA Cup third round), 5 January 1957

'Johnston headed a beautiful goal from White's perfect corner kick.'
Leyton Orient 1 Grimsby Town 1 (Division Two), 12 January 1957

'Johnston scored a magnificent goal from a centre by White.'
Doncaster Rovers 6 Leyton Orient 1 (Division Two), 19 January 1957

'We give the biggest bunch of posies to big blonde centre-forward Tommy Johnston. He doesn't seem to mind how much ground he covers in a game. He's a glutton for hard work – a glutton with a shot like the kick of a mule. He cottoned on to a White corner kick and lashed a thunderbolt into the roof of the net. Then he scored with a beautifully timed flying header, typical of the man, from a Ronnie Heckman cross to equalise against the Second Division runners-up.'
Leyton Orient 2 Stoke City 2 (Division Two), 2 February 1957

'The judgement and understanding between Johnston and his colleagues (Heckman, White and Woosnam) was almost uncanny.'
Middlesbrough 1 Leyton Orient 2 (Division Two), 9 February 1957

'Johnston cleverly diverted Heckman's shot past West Ham's goalie Robinson Wyllie.'
West Ham United 2 Leyton Orient 1 (Division Two), 16 February 1957

'Both Woosnam and Andrews frittered away many opportunities provided by an astute leader in Johnston, whose hard work brought little response from his colleagues.'
Swansea Town 1 Leyton Orient 0 (Division Two), 2 March 1957

'Johnston scored O's third goal with a clever back-header from McKnight's lofted pass.'
Leyton Orient 3 Port Vale 2 (Division Two), 23 March 1957

'After 14 minutes, Orient was one up from a well-taken solo goal by Tommy Johnston.'
Leyton Orient 1 Leicester City 5 (Division Two), 19 April 1957

'Despite the score Johnston had a very good match, he scored two great goals and had another unluckily disallowed in this first game of the season.'
Grimsby Town 7 Leyton Orient 2 (Division Two), 24 August 1957

'If Johnston had faded like Orient's other forwards, Doncaster's defence could have gone home after half-time, but he kept them at it.'
Doncaster Rovers 2 Leyton Orient 0 (Division Two), 28 August 1957

'Both goals scored by Tommy Johnston – one a free kick, smashed home from over 20 yards.'
Leyton Orient 2 Doncaster Rovers 0 (Division Two), 5 September 1957

'Tommy Johnston, who is on West Ham's 'wanted list', schemed Orient to a deserved victory over Cardiff.'
Leyton Orient 4 Cardiff City 2 (Division Two), 14 September 1957

'Already Johnston has brought his goal tally in League games for the season to 11, with this brace – last week he also scored twice at Charlton. He's a great player.'
Leyton Orient 2 Charlton Athletic 2 (Division Two), 19 September 1957

'Forward Tommy Johnston, the 'back room boy' of Leyton Orient's triumph in the last home match, was the grandstand hero against Barnsley. Last week at inside-left, he distracted the Middlesbrough defence while Len Julians scored all four goals. This time he netted both Orient goals to bring his League tally to 14.'
Leyton Orient 2 Barnsley 1 (Division Two), 12 October 1957

'When Johnston headed a beauty into the net, he was unlucky to be flagged offside.'
Fulham 3 Leyton Orient 1 (Division Two), 19 October 1957

'It was tall blonde sharp shooter Tommy Johnston who really clinched the game. Jumping high above the Swansea defence, he headed a brilliant goal in the second half and went onto complete his hat-trick.'
Leyton Orient 5 Swansea Town 1 (Division Two), 26 October 1957

'Tommy Johnston might have had a hat-trick, besides his great goal, he also had two efforts scrambled off the line.'
Ipswich Town 5 Leyton Orient 3 (Division Two), 30 November 1957

'A magnificent display of goalmaking by the big craggy centre-forward Tommy Johnston.'
Leyton Orient 5 Blackburn Rovers 1 (Division Two), 7 December 1957

'Of course, you can't talk about Orient's win – or even talk about Orient at all – without somehow mentioning the name of Tommy Johnston. The craggy Scot who finds it easier to score great goals than to talk about them; the soft-spoken leader who hits the ball as though he loathes leather and is always, in everything, so good. Johnston is a complete master of his trade. Tell that to the Scottish selectors!'
Leyton Orient 5 Grimsby Town 1 (Division Two), 21 December 1957

'The just superb Tommy Johnston scored 4 of the goals in this great display. There's no stopping the fabulous feats of the big Scotsman, and he's after the long-standing record of Dixie Dean's 60 League goals.'
Leyton Orient 6 Rotherham United 2 (Division Two), 25 December 1957

'Hot-shot Tommy Johnston scored another wonder goal on Saturday 26 December 1957, at Rotherham United, to increase his lead as the top goalscorer in the country to 11 goals. Here are the leaders by each Division:
   Division One: Gordon Turner of Luton 20, Bobby Robson of WBA 19, Joe Hayes of Manchester City on 18.
   Division Two: **Tommy Johnston** of Leyton Orient 32, Brian Clough of Middlesbrough 21, George Kelly of Stoke City on 21.

Division Three South: Sam McCrory of Southend United on 20, Wilf Carter of Plymouth Argyle on 19.

Division Three North: Alf Ackerman of Carlisle United on 20, Keith Williams of Tranmere Rovers on 19.' The *Daily Express,* December 1957

'The former Sunderland player and Kilmarnock manager Alex Hastings says that he is not surprised that the former Loanhead boy Tommy Johnston is now top of the goalscoring lists with Leyton Orient.

"I remember centre-forward Tommy coming to Rugby Park six years ago from Peebles Rovers. An outstanding feature of his play was his head work. There was a Jimmy McGrory touch, manner and class about him, in which they both could glide the ball with their heads very powerfully into the net, more powerfully that many could kick a ball. Johnston's a grand player and should be capped by Scotland."'

Authors' Note: This was quite a compliment from Hastings, comparing Tommy Johnston's heading ability to that of Jimmy McGrory. He was the man who scored a record 550 senior goals in British first-class football, most of them for Celtic – a remarkable 397 goals from 378 League games – between 1923 and 1937. Born in Garngad in Scotland on 26 April 1904, McGrory was immensely potent in the air, although only 5ft 8in, and a proportion of his goals were gliding headers. McGrory, although he won seven caps for his country, was largely ignored by the selectors. He was a public relations officer with Celtic until his death in 1982.

'Orient got on terms through a cleverly headed goal by Johnston.' *Stoke City 1 Leyton Orient 3 (Division Two), 28 December 1957*

'You might guess who Orient can thank, yes of course their goalscoring machine, the big bustling Tommy Johnston.' *Leyton Orient 1 Reading 0 (FA Cup, third round), 4 January 1958*

'It's Johnston again, as he chases Derek's and Dixie's records. Let's get away from all the sports talk of sacked managers, and talkative chairmen, and turn the spotlight on a 30-year-old London Scot who's worth more than £30,000 of anybody's money.

Yes, we mean the prince of goal-snatchers Leyton Orient's braw laddie, Tommy Johnston, who scored another rattling hat-trick against Bristol City yesterday. He is after two records. Derek Dooley of Sheffield Wednesday, he chalked up 46 goals from 30 matches and the great Dixie Dean's 60 League goals in 39 matches in 1927–28.

Johnston, who is already on 36 goals from 25 matches, still has 16 games left. We say. Could be done you know, and we for one, would like to see Johnston do it.' *The People* newspaper.
Leyton Orient 4 Bristol City 0 (Division Two), 11 January 1958

'Tommy Johnston was not up to his usual standard, he seemed to be feeling the effects of a leg injury, as his fitness had been in doubt all week.'
Cardiff City 4 Leyton Orient 1 (FA Cup, fourth round), 25 January 1958

'I believe Johnston, now goalless for three weeks, should have had a tremendous header which flew past Tommy Younger allowed in the 83rd minute but referee Arthur Ellis ruled it offside for some reason. Maybe there's a good reason for his loss of goals?'
Leyton Orient 1 Liverpool 0 (Division Two), 1 February 1958

Tommy's days with Blackburn Rovers
'Blackburn have clearly made an excellent capture in Tommy Johnston. He's a top-class goalscorer, leads the attack intelligently and his heading ability is outstanding, scoring two great goals on debut.'
Blackburn Rovers 3 Grimsby Town 0 (Division Two), 8 March 1958

'Tommy Johnston was the brain behind all Rovers' 4 goals – he led the attack brilliantly and only a tremendous save from Orient goalkeeper Frank George prevented him getting onto the score sheet with a fine header.'
Blackburn Rovers 4 Leyton Orient 1 (Division Two), 19 April 1958

'Well, it took a lot of talking by Rovers boss Johnny Carey to get Leyton Orient to part with their hot-shot centre-forward Tommy Johnston, but it certainly paid off, he not only scored eight goals but also made a host of goals for Peter Dobing and Bryan Douglas.' Blackburn Rovers promotion article

'Big Scotsman Johnston topped the Second Division goalscorer's list on 43 League goals, ahead of Middlesbrough's Brian Clough. (He also netted one for Orient, in the FA Cup.) It's the first time in 35 years that a Scot has topped the English League scoring list.' Blackburn Rovers promotion article

Authors' Note: In the 1963–64 season, Scottish-born Hugh McIlmoyle hit 39 League goals for Fourth Division side Carlisle United to top the League charts.

'Tommy Johnston was making his debut in the First Division, he looked very comfortable in this higher class and weighed in with two excellent goals. Johnston always had both eyes on creating chance, for himself or a teammate and he celebrated his long cherished Division One debut with a brace and also made the third.'
Newcastle United 1 Blackburn Rovers 5 (Division One), 22 August 1958

'Spurs' young goalkeeper John Hollowbread was making his League debut, he now knows the First Division has some real potent goal-grabbers. He and the Spurs defence were dazzled by the brilliance of Tommy Johnston.

The Scot, who was giving more than 10 years to Maurice Norman, also gave him a real beating scoring twice in the 27th and 35th minutes and made another for Dobing.'
Blackburn Rovers 5 Tottenham Hotspur 0 (Division One) August 1958

Authors' Note: Maurice Norman was well known to Johnston, Norman was a youngster with Norwich City when Johnston was becoming a star at Carrow Road.

'Johnston did miss a couple of chances later on but it was his goal that gave Rovers the lead at half-time against old club Leyton Orient and he set up the others.'

*Blackburn Rovers 4 Leyton Orient 2 (FA Cup round three), 10
January 1959*

Johnston's second spell with Leyton Orient
'Johnston hasn't scored in his three games since rejoining Orient but
when he's settled in, he will.'
Leyton Orient 1 Liverpool 3 (Division Two), 28 February 1959

'Tommy Johnston headed two fine goals for Orient, Phil White and
Joe Elwood supplied the perfect crosses.'
Sheffield United 2 Leyton Orient 3 (Division Two), 7 March 1959

'Tommy Johnston, who scored one, was the schemer supreme for
Eddie Brown the flashing goal-grabbing speedster with 4 goals to
chalk up 200 League career goals.'
Leyton Orient 6 Sunderland 0 (Division Two), 30 March 1959

'Happy Wanderer Tommy Johnston made sure Orient will stay in
Division Two next season with an excellent goal.'
Bristol City 0 Leyton Orient 1 (Division Two), 18 April 1959

'Tommy Johnston, who shot Blackburn Rovers into the First Division
a year ago, takes most of the credit for booting Barnsley into the
Third with 2 wonderful goals.'
Barnsley 1 Leyton Orient 3 (Division Two), 29 April 1959

'Johnston went storming away to give Orient the lead.'
Bristol Rovers 2 Leyton Orient 2 (Division Two), 22 August 1959

'When Ipswich fought back briefly in the second half Tommy
Johnston ended their flourish with a beautiful header from a Ken
Facey centre.'
Leyton Orient 4 Ipswich Town 1 (Division Two), 29 August 1959

'Even though 2–0 down Orient were full of fight and Tommy

Johnston scored another excellently taken goal from a perfect cross from Elwood in the last minute.'
Stoke City 2 Leyton Orient 1 (Division Two), 2 September 1959

'A fine goal by Tommy Johnston gave Leyton Orient the lead after only 5 minutes of their game with Rotherham United. This goal a pull-down with his right to crack home a scorcher with his left foot, it couldn't have been bettered. The craggy Scotsman looks as good, and deadly as ever.'
Leyton Orient 2 Rotherham United 3 (Division Two), 12 September 1959

'Tommy Johnston delighted the home crowd with some neat touches and setting up goals for the other forwards.'
Leyton Orient 4 Lincoln City 1 (Division Two), 19 September 1959

'Burly Tommy Johnston burst onto the ball to crack a tremendous shot past goalkeeper William Bly from fully 20 yards.'
Leyton Orient 3 Hull City 1 (Division Two), 17 October 1959

'The biggest roar of the day came for big Tommy Johnston who sent one of his old-fashioned power headers flashing home past goalie Peter Taylor, from White's perfect cross eight minutes from time and Brisbane Road erupted. It put the fair-haired Scot two ahead of England and Middlesbrough leader Brian Clough in the Second Division goalscorers' race.

The brilliant Scot actually had a hand in all five of Orient's goals. He also had a goal-bound header fisted off the line by Harris. Ken Facey converting the resulting penalty kick. The veteran craggy Scot outshone Clough throughout the match, showing he is the best centre-forward in the country.'
Leyton Orient 5 Middlesbrough 0 (Division Two), 31 October 1959

'Tommy Johnston was a constant menace to the County rear-guard.'
Derby County 1 Leyton Orient 1 (Division Two), 7 November 1959

'Tommy Johnston the Leyton Orient centre-forward scored two of the three goals in an exciting three minutes at Liverpool. His first gave him his 200th League career goal. It was just brilliant the way he rose to head home from a Terry McDonald cross. Johnston was easily the best player on show at Anfield, he later chalked up his 201st League goal, also a header from another McDonald cross.'
Liverpool 4 Leyton Orient 3 (Division Two), 21 November 1959

'White put over a great centre for Johnston to head in, what's new?'
Bristol City 1 Leyton Orient 1 (Division Two), 5 December 1959

'Toast these great men who typify many... we extend greetings to a group of players who, for us, seem to typify certain qualities found at every football club.

Men such as Tommy Johnston, he remains his old rip-roaring self, a lion in the goal-area and an age-less attacker who has given his best for every one of his seven clubs. All his clubs will testify to his capable match-winning qualities to his endless enthusiasm and 'go'.

Johnston has seen service in many parts of this land, yes: but only because he is the kind of player much sought after by any sensible manager.

To all these colourful characters of the soccer field, we say "A happy Christmas – and thanks for all the memories."

For the record the eight other players included (one in fact was a manager): Denis Hatsell (Preston North End), Ferenc Puskas (Real Madrid), Jimmy Hagan (Peterborough United), Rolando Ugolini (Wrexham), Gerry Harris (Wolverhampton Wanderers), Maurice Setters (West Bromwich Albion), Jimmy Dickinson (Portsmouth) and David Cliss (Chelsea).' *Soccer Star Magazine, 19 December 1959*

'O's lost 2–1 to a last 40 second Roger Hunt 'lucky goal' to Liverpool at Anfield in a FA Cup tie. The ball spun off O's goalie Dave Groombridge's shoulder and rolled back ever so slowly over the line. Orient's greatest star was Tommy Johnston. He inspired a great

Orient rally and he even had the partisan Liverpool's 40,000 odd fans shouting and clapping their approval of his play.'
Liverpool 2 Leyton Orient 1 (FA Cup Third Round), 9 January 1960

'Then came the game's great goal. A flashing Tommy Johnston header from Brown's corner kick, it was Orient's 23rd corner.'
Leyton Orient 2 Huddersfield Town 1 (Division Two), 16 January 1960

'Johnston scored a grand goal, uncharacteristically missed a couple of chances and showed some lovely touches.'
Lincoln City 2 Leyton Orient 2 (Division Two), 6 February 1960

'Centre-forward Tommy Johnston provided a succession of great passes and from one, Orient scored. Johnston was the star of the match and capped a fine performance by notching Orient's fourth goal.'
Sunderland 1 Leyton Orient 4 (Division Two), 20 February 1960

'Orient went ahead after 10 minutes against Cardiff City with a brilliant solo effort by Johnston and then two up with another by the Scot from a White centre.

That old fox Johnston. His first goal, after a run right from the halfway line, was one goal in a thousand, just pure class. Later his delicate header from White's centre was another piece of pure soccer craft.

Johnston, the Hidegkuti of Leyton, London E10, inspired Orient to both subtlety play and goal threat in their impressive opening. Facing his own goal and standing near the half way line, he took a waist high pass from White and made a spectacular goal from it. He turned with the ball balanced on his instep and ran 40 yards to plaster it past Cardiff goalkeeper Graham Vearncombe. Then a mistake by Cardiff's debutante left-half Barry Hole left Johnston free, he set up a triangular move with White and the centre-forward neatly headed in himself and Leyton were 2-up.'

Leyton Orient 3 Cardiff City 4 (Division Two), 27 February 1960
Authors' Note: The reporter was referring to the great Hungarian deep-lying centre-forward Nandor Hidegkuti, a member of the Hungarian side that beat England at Wembley 6–3; he scored a hat-trick that day. He won 69 caps for his country, scoring 39 goals. He died on 14 February 2002, just before his 81st birthday. He was considered to be one of the greatest Hungarian players of all time. It was another compliment for Tommy Johnston to be compared with this great player.

'How Hull could have used a leader with the dash and ball control of Orient's Tommy Johnston. On 28 minutes, he took a through pass, raced on, and calmly lifted the ball over the head of advancing goalkeeper Bernard Fisher.'
Hull City 1 Leyton Orient 2 (Division Two), 5 March 1960

'Tommy Johnston got the second Orient goal with a beautiful header.'
Leyton Orient 2 Liverpool 0 (Division Two), 9 April 1960

'Tommy Johnston got his reward in the 83rd minute with a magnificent header from a free-kick by Ken Facey. Johnston, a more enterprising leader than Brian Clough on the day, headed a great Orient equaliser.'
Middlesbrough 2 Leyton Orient 2 (Division Two), 30 April 1960

'Eddie Brown served up his roving tricks as he came weaving down the left to square inside to Johnston, whose shot rocketed into the roof of the net. More than once, non-stop Johnston had shots blocked, but he never gave up. The big fair-haired centre-forward, he has saved Orient on so many occasions, did it again at Brighton.'
Brighton & Hove Albion 1 Leyton Orient 1 (Division Two), 24 August 1960

'Leyton came back to equalise and then take the lead with goals from Tommy Johnston in the 38th and 42nd minutes. For the first, he tapped the rebound home after Dennis Sorrell hit a post and his second, yet another glorious header from a Phil White cross.

163

Orient's hero was the ace of goal-poachers, Tommy Johnston, who snatched two shock goals within five minutes, so Orient must thank hard-working leader Johnston for the point they took from unbeaten Scunthorpe.'
Scunthorpe United 2 Leyton Orient 2 (Division Two), 27 August 1960

'Tommy Johnston cleverly steered the London boys to their first away win of the season. He snapped the second goal and brilliantly schemed the third for Malcolm Graham. Johnston is still a great powerhouse in League football.'
Leeds United 1 Leyton Orient 3 (Division Two), 7 September 1960

'It was left to veteran Tommy Johnston to rescue the points with a couple of typically well-taken goals, he gave the Derby centre-half Mike Smith a gruelling afternoon.'
Leyton Orient 2 Derby County 1 (Division Two), 10 September 1960

'Tommy Johnston led the Orient attack with more vigour than any of the Bristol forwards.'
Bristol Rovers 4 Leyton Orient 2 (Division Two), 17 September 1960

'Johnston and White set up the first goal for Brown and then Johnston brilliantly headed the second from yet another Phil White cross.'
Stoke City 1 Leyton Orient 2 (Division Two), 8 October 1960

'Never say die Johnston ran through the mud to equalise for Orient.'
Leyton Orient 2 Swansea Town 2 (Division Two), 15 October 1960

'Brown and Johnston worked well in the Orient attack and it was Johnston who grabbed a great winning goal.'
Portsmouth 1 Leyton Orient 2 (Division Two), 5 November 1960

'Tommy Johnston looked good, had a goal disallowed. The wily Scot gave the polished Charlie Hurley a hard afternoon's work but he had little support from his fellow Orient players.'
Sunderland 4 Leyton Orient 1 (Division Two), 19 November 1960

'Best goal of the match, was scored by Johnston. He glided a header past Neil Kennon with devastating judgement and power, from a George Waites centre which reminded the 19,463 fans that although seven years have passed since he left Carrow Road, he is still a past master at heading goals. His general leadership fully justified his appointment as Orient's skipper for the day.'
Norwich City 3 Leyton Orient 2 (Division Two), 3 December 1960

'Tommy Johnston put Orient further ahead after 55 minutes with a brilliant header, this was Orient's first home win since early September and they were inspired by veteran Tommy Johnston. He ploughed his way through thick mud to spray accurate passes to his colleagues. I salute Tommy Johnston.'
Leyton Orient 2 Scunthorpe United 1 (Division Two), 31 December 1960

'Gillingham veteran goalkeeper John Simpson had been tested several times by the craggy Scot before the irrepressible Tommy Johnston headed Orient into the lead on 11 minutes from a Ron Foster cross. The big Scot played deeper and created many open spaces for his colleagues and he had a hand in two other goals.'
Gillingham 2 Leyton Orient 6 (FA Cup round three), 7 January 1961

'Orient came very close to scoring a second goal when Johnston hit a post in this shock Cup win.'
Southampton 0 Leyton Orient 1(FA Cup round four), 28 January 1961

'Poor old Tommy Johnston, he never gave up. Even the Liverpool crowd cheered him off the pitch but all he got out of this game was

a booking by the referee for arguing. What a great centre-forward the old Blackburn player still is. Despite Orient being thrashed, Johnston was the craftiest player on the field, his brilliant touches on the wet pitch brought appreciative gasps from the Liverpool fans.'
Liverpool 5 Leyton Orient 0 (Division Two), 11 February 1961

'Orient leader Tommy Johnston distributed the ball brilliantly, weaving past the Luton defenders to create chances for Alan Sealey and Ron Newman and then Ron Baynham had to leap high to keep out a great Johnston header.'
Leyton Orient 2 Luton Town 1 (Division Two), 11 March 1961

'The ever-dangerous Tommy Johnston came storming in to slide the ball home for a great goal.'
Leyton Orient 3 Stoke City 1 (Division Two), 10 April 1961

'Tommy Johnston got his biggest kick of the season as he lashed onto White's centre and scored a great goal, which keeps Orient in Division Two against old club Norwich. It was cheers all the way, with the O's fans waiting at the end to salute the irrepressible Johnston.'
Leyton Orient 1 Norwich City 0 (Division Two), 22 April 1961

Tommy's debut with Gillingham
'Gillingham's first win of the season came against high-flying Millwall. The win was inspired by new £3,000 signing Tommy Johnston. He led the attack with great skill to transform the eight defeats in a row team. Johnston's debut goal came in the 19th minute and he struck again three minutes later when after a great header Ray Brady, the Millwall defender, could only deflect the ball into his own net, from then on it was Gillingham all the way. Johnston is voted as our player of the match, with a rating of nine out of 10.'
Gillingham 3 Millwall 1 (Division Four), September 1961

Leyton Orient football programme, 3 March 1956, reporting Tommy Johnston's arrival from Newport County.

Johnston in action at Torquay on Easter Monday, 2 April 1956.

18 April 1956. The O's (wearing shirts borrowed from Arsenal) celebrate in the dressing room after their match with Brighton. As well as Tommy (standing, second from right), players Heckman, Welton, Blizzard and Hartburn are in the picture.

Leyton Orient 1955–56, Champions of Division Three South. Standing, left to right: L. Gore (trainer), McMahon, Julians, Earl, Blizzard, J. Mallett (coach), Welton, Johnston, Bishop, Gregory, N. Collins (assistant trainer). Seated: Facey, White, Woosnam, Aldous, A. Stock (manager), McKnight, Heckman, Hartburn, Smith.

Season 1956/7 No. 2.   SEPT. 1956   One Shilling

LEYTON ORIENT
NEWS
ILLUSTRATED

GOAL-MOUTH INCIDENT IN THE BURY MATCH.

Tommy opens the scoring for the O's against Notts County on 13 September 1956. Orient went on to win 3–1.

The letter to the FA from an observer at the game against Doncaster Rovers, in which Johnston was sent off. Tommy was eventually cleared by the FA as a result.

50, Buckhurst Way,
Buckhurst Hill,
Essex.

18th September 1956.

The Secretary,
The Football Association,
22, Lancaster Gate,
London. W.2.

Dear Sir,

Leyton Orient v Doncaster Rovers.
Saturday 15th Sept. 1956

May I as a spectator at the above match be excused writing you, I do feel however that having had a clear view of incidents arising to the sending off of T.Johnston my observations may be of some assistance to you.

At the onset Johnston received a long pass from Gregory outside the Doncaster penalty area and upon turning to feed his right wing was brought down from behind by Williams, the referee immediately stopped play, spoke to both players and awarded a free kick, from that point intimidation was continually taking place until Johnston was sent off.

Previous to the sending off Doncaster were attacking the Orient goal, Johnston and Williams standing approximately at the edge of the centre circle in the Doncaster circle, Johnston moved away from Williams to the Inside Right position and Williams followed (play still being in the Orient penalty area) Johnston again moved into the centre of the pitch and again Williams followed; within a few seconds the ball was cleared from the Orient penalty area and was being brought through by Facey when Williams left Johnston and went for Facey conceding a free kick. The referee neared the spot indicating from where he wished the kick to be taken, by this time Williams had taken up position by the right hand post of the Doncaster goal and immediately alongside Johnston, the ball being placed the whistle was blown, the referee (head down) proceeding towards the Doncaster goal, Facey took the kick and at once the elbow of Williams struck Johnston who was most definately impeded, Johnston reeled and buried his face in his hands and to my amazement the referee pointed to the dressing room. In my humble and unbiased opinion the referee by his posture was in no way in a position to make such a drastic decision.

Fulham v Orient on 8 December 1956. The players pictured are Johnston (Orient), Lampe (Fulham) and Black (Fulham, goalkeeper).

A fruitless Leyton Orient attack from the FA Cup match against Chelsea on 5 January 1957. Johnston is blocked by Reg Matthews. The game ended in a two-goal defeat for the Brisbane Road men.

Doncaster Rovers goalkeeper Harry Gregg collects the ball under pressure from Tommy Johnston, watched by teammate Charlie Williams. The date is 15 September 1956 and the match finished 1-1. Gregg would go on to play for Manchester United and be a survivor of the Munich air crash in 1958, while Williams became nationally known as a stand-up comic in TV's *The Comedians* and many other shows.

Leyton Orient, January 1957. Standing: Willemse, Gregory, Facey, Groombridge, Forbes, Smith. Sitting: White, Sexton, Aldous, Johnston, Heckman.

Leyton Orient v Grimsby Town, 12 January
1957. Tommy Johnston and Dave Sexton are the
Orient players pictured.

ORIENT'S ACE MARKSMAN
TELLS HIS OWN STORY

GOALS GALORE!

by
TOMMY JOHNSTON

Soccer fans all over Britain are asking : " Can Tommy
Johnston, Leyton Orient's crack marksman, beat the
all-time record of ' Dixie ' Dean, the Everton wonder,
who scored 60 League goals in 39 matches ? "

Tommy has a great chance—If he steers clear of injury.

He stands (head and feet) above every other forward in the Football League today
with a total of 35 goals.

Can he do it ? Fifteen matches to go, 26 goals to score ! It's a mighty big task, but
not beyond the powers of this ace centre-forward with the hat-trick habit. Terror
of every goalkeeper, Tommy is the most feared leader in the game today.

What a celebration there will be down Leyton way if this flying Scotsman achieves
his great " goal " — " Dixie " Dean's 30 years-old record !

On-the-target Tommy has had much to do with Orient's big revival and the fans
thrill to his feats.

How does he do it ? What are his goal-getting secrets ? Is he going to smash
that record ?

For the answers, look out for three exciting articles which Tommy has written
exclusively for the " Empire News." The first will appear in tomorrow's

EMPIRE NEWS

Make sure of your Copy—ORDER it on the way home !

A press portrait
of Tommy
Johnston in
Leyton Orient
colours.

Tommy and family visiting Loanhead in the close season, 1957.

Tommy and Phil White with teammates on a boat in Malta, 1956–57 season.

In the garden with Alison and Neil at 32 Durham Avenue, Woodford Green, Essex.

Orient players at the snooker table. From left to right: Dennis Sorrell, Cyril Lea, George Waites, Terry McDonald, Phil White, Tommy Johnston, Stan Charlton, Joe Elwood and Ken Facey with the cue.

Scoring for Leyton Orient against Grimsby Town on 21 December 1957. Orient won the match 5–1.

The sequence of photographs taken by photographer Bob Stiggins at the Grimsby Town game showing Tommy's heading technique.

LEAP AND A TWIST AND A SCORCHING HEADER FROM

e News Chronicle rapid-sequence camera spotlights the skill of a ss centre-forward. Facing his own goal, challenged by Grimsby's Bill own, Tom Johnston of Leyton Orient soars to a centre, twists in mid- air, and speeds the ball past goalkeeper Clarence Williams for t of a hat-trick. It's the sort of chance that can be missed without the sort of chance Johnston specialises in . . . Pictures by Bob

.. AND IT'S ANOTHER GOAL FOR LEYTON ORIENT'S FLYING S

Leyton Orient in 1959 wearing the hats sent to them by Pat Boone. From left to right: Joe Elwood, Tommy Johnston, Dave Groombridge, Eddie Brown, Stan Charlton, Ronnie Foster, Les Gore, Ken Facey, Terry McDonald, Sid Bishop, Nick Collins, Alan Eagles, Dennis Sorrell.

Signing for Blackburn Rovers in 1957–58.

A photograph of the Johnstons at home taken for an article in a magazine.

Tommy's first goal for Blackburn Rovers against Grimsby.

Chapter 13

What the fans said

Over the years Tommy Johnston has received literally hundreds of letters from supporters of the various clubs he played for. Below are just a few extracts from some of the letters. Tommy still has the originals.

Dear Tommy,
I am 'The Scout' of the *Glasgow Evening News* and I would like to give you a write up this week, as I feel you deserve it seeing you are doing so well in goalscoring for the Canaries.

I have always felt that Kilmarnock made a blunder in giving you a 'free' and I know you will be interested to know that Alex Hastings, their former manager, who signed you for Killie is a personal friend of mine and he shares the same opinion. If you are phoning me be sure and transfer the charge.

      John Begg
      22 September 1952

Dear Tommy
I hope you will excuse the liberty I am taking writing to you, but I am wondering about certain questions and I sincerely wish you will try your best to answer them.

My friend and I have watched your progress very eagerly since you left the 'Latics'. One of the questions we have given up answering years ago trying to answer is why did the Latics ever let you go in the first place? As the Americans say, this is the '64 million dollar question'.

> Steve Johnson
> Failsworth
> 15 September 1953

Dear Tommy

Just a short letter to thank you most sincerely for the letter you sent me in reply to my questions. You answered them very truthfully and your career will be followed more closely than ever now.

My friend simply devoured every word you wrote when he read it. It is surprising how a small thing like a letter from a professional footballer can make a lot of people very happy indeed.

Once again Tommy thank you very much indeed and all the very best for the future.

> Steve Johnson
> Failsworth
> 21 October 1953

Dear Tommy,

First, let me congratulate you on your most wonderful performance at Highbury last Saturday, also your teammates'. Would you please send me your signed autograph and a photograph, as I have always been a great supporter and admirer of your football skill.

Your achievements will live forever in our history.

> Peter Thurtle
> Holt, Norfolk
> 1 February 1954

Dear Sir,

As an Arsenal fan but one who believes in giving praise where it is due, I want to congratulate you on your fine performance and your team upon your fine victory on Saturday.

I send my best wishes for your every success in the future.

> P.M. Pooley
> Cirencester
> 7 February 1954

Dear Mr Johnston

I am happy to inform you that you have been awarded an engraved Ronson lighter for your outstanding performance in the FA Cup at Highbury, against Arsenal.

Congratulations on your achievement.

> W.T. Mann
> Editor
> *Sporting Record Weekly*
> 10 February 1954

Dear Tommy,

I am a regular supporter of Newport County and I would like to express my appreciation of your play whilst with our club. I am sorry you will not been seen in the black and amber colours again, I'm sure County's goal average will suffer.

However, nothing can alter the fact that another club will be benefiting from your play and I should like to wish you all the best of luck in your first full season with Leyton Orient.

Newport County's loss is Orient's gain and I hope the supporters there will get as much enjoyment from your 90-minute play as I did when watching you at Somerton Park.

Once more, I wish you a good season in the Second Division.

> R. Walters
> Newport
> 13 August 1956

Dear Mr Johnston,

I am writing to thank you for the great kindness to an old man last Saturday. I asked if you could put me in touch with someone who could give me a seat. When I told you I was 84 years old and could not stand for long owing to illness, you said would see what you could do.

Well, immediately you came out with a ticket for the stand. I appreciate your kindness very much. I cannot insult you by giving you a small gift, but I can wish you every success in the future and freedom from serious injury.

I have followed the O's since they were formed as amateurs in the 1890s and have not missed many matches. The team has a great chance for promotion and I want to see them in Division Two.

I must close with again thanking you for your great kindness, which I enjoyed very much. Up the O's.

> F. Langley
> Clapton
> 2 April 1956

Dear Sir,

Just a line to congratulate you on your display against Fulham on Saturday. Rarely have I seen a better goal than the one you scored in the first half a clever piece of anticipation, which left the Fulham goalkeeper standing.

Wishing all the best in your future games.

> An Orient Supporter
> December 1956

Dear Mr Johnston

When you played against Orient for Newport County, I said to my friends in the stand 'We could do with that man Johnston, he is an intelligent goalscoring player.'

Sir, you are still just that.

> Leslie Smith
> Woodford Green
> Essex
> 18 September 1956

Dear Tom,

Keep up the good spirit in soccer and for the festive season. Tom, keep that smile upon your face it's a tonic to others, but you don't know it.

I work as a Theatre Porter in a Children's Hospital and I love my job so if you would like to pop in and have a couple of sherries, you are welcome, then you can sign the photo I have of you from a recent soccer annual. The best of luck to you Tom in everything.

> Harry McCann
> Victoria
> 15 December 1957

Dear Mr Johnston,

May I send a brief word of congratulations as you progress in your astounding run of goals this season. I have seen your play at Swindon and I have always admired your style.

Your present success does remind me of our one-time star centre-forward Harry Morris. (He was also with Clapton Orient). So here's the very best of luck you deserve, may you smash all records this season. (What about signing for Swindon??? !!!!)

> Bill Paul
> Swindon, Wilts
> 30 December 1957

Dear Mr Johnston,

A very brief note wishing you and all the lads a very successful day in Wales next Saturday. In this evening's *Standard* they say your legs are getting better, let's hope it is true and that you get a couple with your 'nut'.

Wishing all the very best and a hat full of goals.

> W.R. Bexon
> Leatherhead, Surrey
> 21 January 1958

Authors' Note: (Tommy Johnston played but was not fully fit, Orient lost 4–1 at Cardiff City in the FA Cup).

Dear Tommy,

May I offer you my sincerest congratulations on your hat-trick against Bristol City on Saturday. I can assure you that you still have a great many friends in Kilmarnock who follow your career with a great deal of interest and we hope you will add considerably to your present total of 35 League goals.

Would you believe at my office on a Monday morning the main topic of conversation is how many goals did you score and may you have a good run until the end of the season.

> Tom Miller
> Kilmarnock
> 12 January 1958

Dear Mr Johnston,

Thank you very much for the autographs of Blackburn Rovers FC. It was very good of you to take the trouble. I hope before long I shall be able to see you play. I am interested in football and I play for my school.

> Robert Bush
> Loughton
> Essex
> 24 May 1958

Dear Tom,

I am a very keen Blackburn Rovers supporter, which is now my favourite team. Leyton Orient used to be my favourite team but when my favourite player was transferred I changed and followed you.

I would be pleased if you could autograph the enclosed photographs and return them to me. Please don't think I am cheeky because if you do please forgive me. I, like you was also born in Scotland at Fifeshire.

> David Dumbar
> Newcastle upon Tyne
> October 1958

Dear Mr Johnston,

I am a keen Blackburn Rovers supporter and I would like very much, like everyone else to see you score some goals again. It is just one of those things but don't give up on courage.

Between you and I, late last season my Husband and I sent Mr Carey a 'good luck' charm to help him find a good centre-forward and luckily he found you, and you got us out of the Second Division so you must be alright.

Best wishes for you to score again and I'm sure it will be on Saturday. Here's hoping.

> Mrs C. Bottomley
> Blackburn
> 9 November 1958

Authors' Note: Tommy Johnston did score a goal the following Saturday in a 3–2 win at West Bromwich Albion on 15 November.

Dear Tom,

I wish to offer you my deepest sympathy in not being able to have any good luck at the moment, which you deserve, I watched you in the last two matches and the luck was still against you.

I was reading Brian Clough's column in last weeks sports paper and he mentions many players are superstitious in various ways so all in good faith I'm going to ask you to try this.

So, take off your bandage from your arm and throw it in the fire, before you go on the field at the Albion, change your bootlaces over to the opposite boot for this match and I'm sure you will score, I say for the future, leave the laces in the same boots and forget about your bandage.

Over 40 years a Rovers fan and I'm 65 in a few weeks.

Yours with best wishes

> Jack Ellis
> Derby
> 12 November 1958

Authors' Note: Tommy never changed his laces, nor took his bandage off, but he did score in Rovers 3–2 win at West Brom.

Dear Tommy

Hope you don't mind us writing to you. Ever since you left Orient we have followed Blackburn and we all miss you terribly. Our first thought on a Saturday is: How did Blackburn do and how many goals did our Tom get?

We have collected every cutting from last season of you and have placed them in a scrapbook. We have never had a greater moment than when the final whistle went in your promotion game at Charlton, but if only you could have scored.

We shall be watching you when the Blackburn team next comes to London at Chelsea and Spurs, we all hope you go on and beat Dixie Dean's record of 60 League goals.

All good luck for the future and hope to hear from you soon.

> Barrie and Graham Hobbins
> (Sons of the former Orient Chief Scout Sid Hobbins)
> Shooters Hill
> Woolwich
> December 1958

Dear Tom,

My young son Stephen and I are great followers of the Orient and felt that congratulations are in order to you in scoring your double century of League goals. I'm sure the game at Liverpool was an absolute cracker and you will surely have just cause in remembering it.

I have followed the O's for over 20 years and can honestly say that the football the boys are playing this season is the best ever.

Please give best wishes to Ken Facey and the boys for their wonderful efforts. The best of luck, Tom.

> J.W. Bennett
> Upminster
> Essex
> 22 November 1959

Dear Mr Johnston,

Please permit me to offer you my heartiest congratulations upon your scoring your 200th and 201st goal as a professional League footballer. May you enjoy the plaudits of the crowd and critics.

Every good wish for freedom of injury and many more 'into the net'.

> James A. Darby
> Hackney
> 22 November 1959

Dear Tommy,

I hope you don't mind me calling you Tommy, for as an Orient supporter for over 40 years you are all Christian names to me. We must admit that things are not going so well for us at present and I was wondering if you remember a few seasons back when things were very much the same.

I believe it was Alec Stock who moved you to inside-left and what a great move it turned out to be and I think one of your first games in that position was against Cardiff City in September 1957 at Leyton, which we won 4–2.

Not to mention a 'goal' by you that brought the house down so to speak and nearly caused a riot when the Referee disallowed it for your hat-trick.

Goals became more plentiful over the following weeks, so what about it Tommy surely it be worth another try to play in a deeper role?

> R.H.
> Leyton
> 1959

Dear Tom,

Just a few lines so I can include the press cutting from the *Liverpool Echo* and the *Daily Post* which you can read for yourself about your wonderful performance Saturday.

I don't know how you do it Tom but you always seem to have such a great game when you play at Anfield. Hope you don't mind me writing but all the very best for weeks ahead.

> Brian Barker
>
> Liverpool

Authors' Note: Liverpool beat Orient 5–0 and yet the Liverpool supporter still wrote to Tommy about his great performance.

Dear Tommy Johnston,

Sir, I wish to thank you as an Orient supporter for over 40 years for the great help and skill that you gave to them. Since you came to us, we have had many thrills – the Third Division championship and your winning goal that settled the issue, some runs in the FA Cup and many magnificent goals.

I would like to wish you every success at Gillingham and I hope you get some goals tomorrow in your debut. Good luck, Sir and thank you again.

> George Wheatley
>
> Leytonstone
>
> 21 September 1961

Authors' Note: Tommy did score on his debut in a 3–1 win over Millwall, it was Gillingham's first win in nine games.

Tribute from an O's fan, to be sung to the tune of the song *Davy Crockett*:

> Came to Leyton Orient from Newport way
> Gives us a thrill when we watch him play
> He's the same home or away
> Bangs them in every Saturday
> Tommy, Tommy Johnston
> The pride of the Orient.
>
> > Frank Kaye
> >
> > Essex

Chapter 14

Great heading ability and much more...

Tommy Johnston was a brilliant goal-scoring centre-forward, as we have seen, but he had many other strengths as well. He was extremely useful at leading an attack and had astute distribution. His ability as a schemer or forager is well documented and he had a hard right-footed kick. He would run for 90 minutes, even in the most terrible of conditions. He was strong and could give and take the hard knocks. He made incisive forward runs that culminated in powerful shots. He was often compared in the press to the great hot shot of the sixties, Arthur Rowley.

Tommy was occasionally criticised for being slow, but this was unfair. He could run 30 to 40 yards with the ball and score, often outpacing defenders. He was able to score all types of goals: headers from the right, left or even behind; drives from 20 or 30 yards; and goals from free-kicks. He could run from deep or dribble past one or two defenders. He scored magnificent close-in goals where good positional play or alertness were required, as well as volleys and even some hook shots.

However, his unique heading ability was without doubt his greatest asset. He could turn what seemed like very difficult chances into goals. He had perfect timing when crosses came over and, in many instances, he was frequently able to reach the ball before any defender.

Only two other players, Dixie Dean and Tommy Lawton, could match Johnston's ability with his head. There have been other good headers of a ball but they are not quite comparable to Tommy Johnston. This may sound like a sweeping statement; however, having checked all the match reports, not even a handful of Orient players in nearly 70 years were described by reporters in such glowing terms as Johnston.

The reports and records relating to Dixie Dean and Tommy Lawton indicate that they were good at a certain type of header, mainly using the front of the forehead. This is the powerful nodded type. Johnston, however, was brilliant from all angles. It didn't matter whether the crosses came from the left or the right, were short or even from behind, they still found the net. In practice, Tommy's great understanding with Phil White meant that the majority of his headers came from right-wing crosses.

William Ralph 'Dixie' Dean

William Dean was known to dislike his nickname of Dixie, given to him by his Everton colleagues because of his very curly and wiry hair, which was like that of the black slaves of the American south.

Born in Birkenhead on 21 January 1907, after school he joined the Wirral Railways as an apprentice. He then joined Tranmere Rovers and scored 27 goals from 27 appearances. In 1934 he joined Everton for £3,000. He spent 13 years with the Toffees, scoring 349 goals from 399 League matches. He scored a record 60 League goals in just 39 games in the 1927–28 season, and he also netted 22 Cup goals, giving him a total for the season of 82 goals.

Later, he had short spells with Notts County and Sligo Rovers in Ireland.

He netted a career total of 473 senior goals from 502 games, including a record 37 hat-tricks. Matt Busby once said of Dean that he could out-jump, out-time and out-head any defender. Fifty percent of his goals came from headers. He collapsed and died while watching Everton play Liverpool in 1980.

Matt Busby, who followed Tommy Johnston's career with great interest, soon saw Dixie Dean's great heading ability in Johnston's own heading technique, which was quite a compliment for the craggy Scot from Loanhead.

Tommy Lawton

Tommy Lawton was born in Bolton on 6 October 1919. Dixie Dean took Lawton under his wing when Lawton joined Everton as a 17-year-old from Burnley in 1937 for a record fee of £6,500. However, his career was interrupted by the outbreak of World War Two. He then had a long career with Chelsea, Notts County, Brentford and Arsenal.

A little-known fact about Lawton is that Leyton Orient nearly signed him twice during his career. During November 1947 he held talks with Leyton Orient to discuss joining the O's for a club record fee from Chelsea, but instead he decided to move to Notts County for £17,500 along with Irish wingman Bill Dickson. In 1951 the O's again tried to sign Lawton to team up with the other former international players on the club's books – Jimmy Blair, Tommy Brown and Billy Rees – but the deal fell through.

As a youngster, Lawton showed the football world that he was a brilliant and powerful header of a ball with two good feet and a blistering turn of pace. He scored a total of 215 League goals from 365 appearances. He died of pneumonia at his Nottingham home on 6 November 1996.

George Arthur Rowley

Born in Wolverhampton on 21 April 1926, Arthur Rowley had an powerful left foot in post-war English football and scored a remarkable 434 goals from 619 League matches. These goals were scored over 19 years, between 1946 and 1965 and with four different clubs: West Bromwich Albion, Fulham, Leicester City and Shrewsbury Town.

His League goalscoring record is unlikely ever to be broken. Rowley died in December 2002, aged 76.

Thirty-four percent of Johnston's goals for Leyton Orient were headers

The authors estimate that 48 of Tommy Johnston's 121 League goals for Leyton Orient were headers, representing a total of 34 percent, many being described as superb efforts. There are too many to describe in detail, but there are five that epitomise his sheer class.

The first example was for Newport County against Leyton Orient at Brisbane Road in a midweek afternoon match on 17 March 1955. The background was that Orient were involved in a promotion struggle with Bristol City, and an O's win would have put them within a point of City with two games in hand. Tommy Johnston was playing for Newport, and he played a big part in the visitors' surprise 2–1 victory. He scored their first goal when the ball came over from the right – it wasn't a very good cross as it was behind Johnston and fairly low, but somehow he reached it with his head and put it in the corner of the net past a surprised Pat Welton. The O's missed their chance to close the gap on City and eventually finished second in the table. Only one club was promoted in those days. How Johnston managed to get to the ball and head home from such an inaccurate low cross only he knows.

The second headed goal was against Grimsby Town in a Division Two match on 21 December 1957. What better way to show off all of Johnston's high-class heading ability and power than the leap and twist and scorching headed goal captured in a series of pictures taken by the *News Chronicle*'s Bob Stiggins with his rapid-sequence camera (see p176 Chapter 12). The reporter wrote:

> *Facing his own goal and challenged by Grimsby's Bill Brown. He soars and twists in mid-air to speed the ball past Clarence Williams for the start of his hat-trick. It's the sort of chance that can be missed without blame, the sort of chance Johnston specialises in and its another goal for Leyton Orient's flying Scot.*

The sports editor of the *News Chronicle* sent the following letter, along with the photographs, to Tommy Johnston:

Dear Tommy,

Here is a good sequence of one of your great goals, which have been making the headlines this season. I thought you might like it for your scrapbook. Keep up the good work.

John Camkin

Sports Editor

A third great header was actually disallowed, and thus did not count in Tommy's goal tally, but it was such a colossus of a goal that referee Ellis's decision could not take away its greatness. Had it counted it would have been considered one of the greatest headers ever in the history of the game. The match was Leyton Orient versus Liverpool in a Division Two fixture on 1 February 1958 at Brisbane Road. Liverpool had penned O's in for a spell but a quick ball was sent up to Phil White on the halfway line. White moved forward a few yards and put over one of his superb crosses. Johnston came steaming in from the left and was in full flight when he met the ball with his left side of his head just outside of the corner of the penalty area. The ball crashed past the Liverpool goalkeeper Tommy Younger from fully 20 yards. The roar of the crowd was stifled as he was judged to have been offside, but it was a fantastic effort.

The fourth example of Johnston's heading genius was in the Leyton Orient versus Brighton & Hove Albion match on 14 March 1959 at Brisbane Road. The O's were struggling and the visiting defence was difficult to penetrate. The O's were awarded a free kick and wily Eddie Baily floated his kick over to the left of the penalty area where Johnston was standing with opposition defenders all around him, including the six-foot tall defender Roy Jennings. Baily's kick was accurate but seemed likely to end in a knockdown in the box. Even though Johnston could not get any leverage on the ball, he rose among the Brighton defenders without being able to move and managed to nod in a beautifully angled headed goal with the ball dipping just under the bar, a goal which was later described in the press as 'sheer class'.

The fifth and final example was also exceptional. Tommy himself thinks it was his greatest-ever goal for Orient, and it was scored shortly after his father's death.

The match was a Division Two fixture against Huddersfield Town on 16 January 1960 at Brisbane Road. The O's won a corner kick on the right and with Phil White absent through injury, Eddie Brown took the corners. The kick appeared far too short and looked as though it was not going to reach the centre of the penalty area. Johnston rushed forward in the crowded penalty area in an attempt to reach the ball, along with two Huddersfield defenders. He had to stoop low and lean slightly back, as the ball dropped to hip height and was about to be kicked away. He managed to stoop between the two defenders and, despite leaning forward in the most awkward of positions, he twisted his head and sent the ball crashing into the net from about 10 yards. It was a goal of the highest quality. The Huddersfield defenders and many O's fans were shaking their heads in disbelief: they couldn't believe what they had just witnessed.

Dozens of other examples could have been used to illustrate Johnston's amazing ability in the air.

Some of the great post-World War Two headers in English League football are: Tommy Lawton, Tommy Taylor (Manchester United), John Charles, Ron Davies, Mark Hateley, Pat Terry, Wyn Davies, Tony Hateley, Maurice Owen, Duncan Ferguson, Frank Stapleton, Bob Latchford, Dion Dublin, Joe Jordan, Alan Shearer and Jim Fryatt. Leyton Orient header specialists include the likes of: Mickey Bullock, Tony Biggs, Dave Dunmore, Ted Phillips, Mark Cooper, Joe Mayo, Gordon Bolland, Colin West, Vic Groves, Dennis Pacey, Kevin Nugent, Vic Halom, Mike Burgess, Len Julians, Billy Rees, Frank Neary and Billy Jennings.

Among all these players we believe that, along with Dean and Lawton, Tommy Johnston was the greatest of them all.

Some of Tommy Johnston's greatest headed goals for Orient as witnessed by the authors

The following is a list of the top 15 headers, ranked in order of merit:

1. v Huddersfield Town   (h) 16 January 1960
2. v Brighton & Hove Albion   (h) 14 March 1959
3. v Barnsley   (h)   3 November 1956
4. v Swansea Town   (h) 26 October 1957
5. v Grimsby Town   (h) 21 December 1957
6. v Bristol City   (h) 11 January 1958
7. v Middlesbrough   (h) 31 October 1959
8. v Bristol City   (a)   5 December 1959
9. v Port Vale   (h) 23 March 1957
10. v Scunthorpe United   (h) 31 December 1960
11. v Ipswich Town   (h) 29 August 1959
12. v Cardiff City   (h) 27 February 1960
13 v Swindon Town   (a) 25 February 1956
14 v Notts County   (h) 23 November 1957
15. v Brighton & Hove Albion   (h) 10 September 1959

Some of Tommy Johnston's greatest headed goals, not witnessed by the authors

These are ranked in order of merit according to Press reports:

1. v Sheffield United   (a)   7 March 1959
2. v Liverpool   (a) 21 November 1959
3. v Norwich City   (a)   3 December 1960
4. v Stoke City   (a) 28 December 1957
5. v Scunthorpe United   (a) 27 August 1960
6. v Fulham   (a)   8 December 1956
7. v Stoke City   (h)   2 February 1957
8. v Aldershot   (h) 17 March 1956
9. v Rotherham United   (h) 17 November 1956
10. v Middlesbrough   (a)   9 February 1957
11. v Stoke City   (a)   8 October 1960
12. v Notts County   (h) 27 April 1957
13. v Grimsby Town   (a) 21 April 1959
14. v Stoke City   (a) 22 September 1956
15. v Middlesbrough   (a) 30 April 1960

Great goals with his feet

Although Tommy Johnston was scoring outstanding goals with his head, he hit many fine strikes with his feet and these are sometimes overlooked. The one pictured below, versus Grimsby Town on 21 December 1957, was photographed by Bob Stiggins. Other memorable shots with his feet were scored in the 1959–60 season, against Rotherham United, Hull City and Cardiff City. These and many others were described as 'brilliant' in the press reports.

Chapter 15

English and Scottish League all-time leading goalscorers, 1888–2004

The records show that Tommy Johnston scored a total of 239 League goals throughout his career. He is currently ranked joint-53rd in the all-time leading League goalscorers list since Football League matches began in 1888. Approximately 38,000 players up to February 2004 (with approximately 8,000 of all these players being forwards or, in today's modern game, strikers) have made an appearance in the Football League.

Below is a ranking of the greatest English Football League goalscorers. Unfortunately, no official listing could be traced, and the following names were located from various sources. The list shows that Tommy Johnston ranks among the very best in the Football League since 1888. The authors apologise if any player has inadvertently been left out of the list.

English League's all-time leading goalscorers between 1888 and season 2003–04

Name	Goals	Career	Clubs
Arthur Rowley	434	1946–64	WBA, Fulham, Leicester, Shrewsbury
William 'Dixie' Dean	379	1923–38	Tranmere, Everton, Notts County
Jimmy Greaves	357	1957–70	Chelsea, Tottenham, West Ham
Steve Bloomer	352	1892–13	Derby County, Middlesbrough, Derby County
George Camsell	345	1924–39	Durham City, Middlesbrough
John Aldridge	330	1979–98	Newport, Oxford, Liverpool, Tranmere
John Atyeo	315	1950–65	Portsmouth, Bristol City
Joe Smith	315	1908–28	Bolton, Stockport
Vic Watson	312	1920–36	West Ham, Southampton
Harry Bedford	308	1919–34	Nottingham Forest, Blackpool, Derby, Newcastle, Sunderland, Bradford PA, Chesterfield
Harry Johnson	307	1919–35	Sheffield Utd, Mansfield Town
Hughie Gallacher	296	1925–39	Newcastle, Chelsea, Derby County, Notts County, Grimsby, Gateshead
Gordon Hodgson	294	1925–39	Liverpool, AstonVilla, Leeds
Cliff Holton	292	1950–67	Arsenal, Watford, Northampton, Crystal Palace, Watford, Charlton, Orient
Jimmy Hampson	290	1925–37	Nelson, Blackpool
Ray Crawford	289	1957–71	Portsmouth, Ipswich, Wolves, WBA, Ipswich, Charlton, Colchester
David 'Harry Abe' Morris	289	1920–34	Fulham, Brentford, Millwall, Swansea, Swindon, Orient
Ernie Hine	288	1921–37	Barnsley, Leicester, Huddersfield, Manchester Utd, Barnsley
Tom Keetley	284	1919–34	Derby County, Bradford PA, Doncaster, Notts County, Lincoln
Arthur Chandler	281	1920–36	QPR, Leicester, Notts County
Ronnie Allen	276	1946–64	Port Vale, WBA, Crystal Palace

Name	Goals	Career	Clubs
George Brown	276	1921–37	Huddersfield, Aston Villa, Burnley, Leeds, Darlington
Ron Davies	275	1959–76	Chester, Luton, Norwich, Southampton, Portsmouth, Manchester Utd, Millwall
Roger Hunt	269	1959–71	Liverpool, Bolton
Ken Wagstaff	269	1960–75	Mansfield Town, Hull City
Kevin Hector	267	1962–81	Bradford Park Avenue, Derby County
Alan Shearer	266	1987–2004	Southampton, Blackburn, Newcastle
Ted Harper	263	1923–34	Blackburn, Sheffield Wednesday, Tottenham, Preston, Blackburn
Bryan 'Pop' Robson	263	1964–84	Newcastle, West Ham, Sunderland, West Ham, Sunderland, Carlisle, Chelsea, Carlisle, Sunderland
David Jack	260	1920–33	Plymouth, Bolton, Arsenal
Charlie Buchan	258	1910–27	Sunderland, Arsenal
Jimmy Cookson	256	1925–37	Chesterfield, WBA, Plymouth, Swindon
Ted MacDougall	256	1967–80	York, Bournemouth, Manchester Utd, West Ham, Norwich, Southampton, Bournemouth, Blackpool
Tommy Briggs	255	1947–58	Grimsby, Coventry, Birmingham, Blackburn, Grimsby
Nat Lofthouse	255	1946–60	Bolton Wanderers
Keith Edwards	254	1975–91	Sheffield Utd, Hull, Sheffield Utd, Leeds, Hull, Stockport, Huddersfield, Plymouth
Tommy Tynan	254	1975–92	Swansea, Sheffield Wednesday, Lincoln, Newport, Plymouth, Rotherham, Plymouth, Rotherham, Plymouth, Torquay, Doncaster
Charlie Wayman	254	1946–57	Newcastle, Southampton, Preston, Middlesbrough, Darlington
Steve Bull	252	1985–99	WBA, Wolves
Ivor Allchurch	251	1947–67	Swansea, Newcastle, Cardiff, Swansea

Name	Goals	Career	Clubs
Brian Clough	251	1955–64	Midddlesbrough, Sunderland
Joe Bradford	250	1920–36	Birmingham City, Bristol City
Harry Hampton	248	1904–23	Aston Villa, Birmingham, Newport County
Ian Rush	246	1978–99	Chester, Liverpool, Leeds, Newcastle, Sheffield Utd, Wrexham
Tom Bamford	245	1928–39	Wrexham, Manchester Utd, Swansea
Geoff Bradford	245	1949–63	Bristol Rovers
Ernie Moss	244	1968–88	Chesterfield, Peterborough, Mansfield, Chesterfield, Port Vale, Lincoln, Doncaster, Chesterfield, Stockport, Scarborough, Rochdale
Tom 'Pongo' Waring	244	1927–39	Tranmere, Aston Villa, Barnsley, Wolves, Tranmere, Accrington
Teddy Sheringham	244	1983–2004	Millwall, Aldershot, Nottingham Forest, Tottenham, Manchester Utd, Tottenham, Portsmouth
George Beel	243	1919–33	Lincoln, Merthyr, Chesterfield, Burnley, Lincoln, Rochdale
Gordon Turner	243	1950–63	Luton Town
David Halliday	241	1925–34	Sunderland, Arsenal, Man City, Orient
Tommy Johnston	**239**	**1951–61**	**Darlington, Oldham, Norwich, Newport, Orient, Blackburn, Orient, Gillingham**
Richard 'Dixie' McNeil	239	1966–83	Exeter, Northampton, Lincoln, Hereford, Wrexham, Hereford

Additional notes, English League:

- Some sources show Arthur Rowley's total as being 433 goals.
- Hughie Gallacher also scored 90 goals for Airdrie, which brings his overall total to 386 goals.
- David Halliday, a former Clapton Orient man, also scored 90 goals for Dundee, which gives him a total of 331 goals.
- Both Alan Shearer's and Teddy Sheringham's statistics are as at June 2004. As at

3 October 2004, Shearer's record had increased by a further three League goals for Newcastle United, and Sheringham's had increased by a further six goals for West Ham United.

- John Aldridge also scored 33 goals for Real Sociedad.
- Jimmy Greaves also scored nine goals for AC Milan.
- Kevin Hector also scored 40 goals for Vancouver Whitecaps.
- Ian Rush also scored seven goals for Juventus.
- Teddy Sheringham also scored 13 goals for Djurgardens.
- Keith Edwards also scored two goals for Aberdeen.
- David Halliday also scored an unknown number of goals for St Mirren 1919–21.
- Often forgotten is regional wartime football. The most prolific goalscorer in wartime football in England between 1939 and 1946 was Albert Stubbins, who scored 245 goals from 199 games for Newcastle United. He also scored four goals in 26 League appearances before the war. He moved to Liverpool in September 1946, scoring a further 77 League goals from 159 League appearances. His career total was 326 goals.
- Tommy Johnston also scored 17 Scottish League goals for Kilmarnock.

All-time leading English League goalscorers (seasonal record) between 1888 and 2004

Player	Total	Club(s)	Season
William 'Dixie' Dean	60	Everton	1927–28
George Camsell	59	Middlesbrough	1926–27
Ted Harston	55	Mansfield Town	1936–37
Joe Payne	55	Luton Town	1936–37
Terry Bly	52	Peterborough United	1960–61
Clarrie Bourton	49	Coventry City	1931–32
Tom 'Pongo' Waring	49	Aston Villa	1930–31
David 'Harry Abe' Morris	47	Swindon Town	1926–27
Alf Lythgoe	46	Stockport County	1933–34
Derek Dooley	46	Sheffield Wednesday	1951–52
Peter Simpson	46	Crystal Palace	1930–31
Jimmy Hampson	45	Blackpool	1929–30
Kevin Hector	44	Bradford Park Avenue	1965–66

Player	Total	Club(s)	Season
Arthur Rowley	44	Leicester City	1956–57
Tom Bamford	44	Wrexham	1933–34
William 'Dixie' Dean	44	Everton	1931–32
Albert Whitehurst	44	Rochdale	1926–27
Jimmy Cookson	44	Chesterfield	1925–26
Brian Clough*	43	Middlesbrough	1958–59
Tommy Johnston	**43**	**Leyton Orient & Blackburn Rovers**	
			1957–58
Frank Newton	43	Fulham	1931–32
David Halliday	43	Sunderland	1928–29
Andrew Rennie	43	Luton Town	1928–29
Ted Harper	43	Blackburn Rovers	1925–26

* Some books show that Brian Clough scored 42 goals in the 1958–59 season. The book by Breedon Publishing *The Complete Record of Middlesbrough FC* shows that Clough scored 43 League goals in the 1958–59 season.

The most recent player to get close to 43 goals in a season was Guy Whittingham for Portsmouth with 42 goals in the 1992–93 season. The highest total in the Premiership thus far is 34, achieved by both Andy Cole and Alan Shearer.

Scottish League's all-time leading goalscorers

Player	Total	Season	Club(s)
Jimmy McGrory	410	1922–38	Celtic, Clydebank, Celtic
Bob McPhail	305	1923–39	Airdrie, Arthurlie, Airdrie, Rangers
Hugh Ferguson	285	1916–30	Motherwell, Dundee
Ally McCoist	282	1978–2001	St Johnstone, Rangers, Kilmarnock
Willie Reid	275	1904–22	Morton, Third Lanark, Motherwell, Rangers, Albion Rovers
Gordon Wallace	264	1963–80	Montrose, Raith Rovers, Dundee, Dundee United, Raith Rovers
Willie McFadyen	260	1921–37	Motherwell, Bo'ness, Clyde, Motherwell
Bob Ferrier	255	1917–37	Motherwell
Jimmy McColl	255	1913–31	Celtic, Partick Thistle, Hibernian

Player	Total	Season	Club(s)
David Wilson	254	1928–39	Hamilton
Willie Wallace	245	1958–75	Stenhousemuir, Raith, Hearts, Celtic, Dumbarton
David McLean	239	1907–32	Celtic, Third Lanark, Rangers, Dundee, Forfar
Andy Cunningham	237	1909–29	Kilmarnock, Rangers

Additional notes, Scottish League:

- Ferguson also netted a further 77 goals with Cardiff City, totalling 362 goals.
- Willie Wallace also scored four goals for Crystal Palace, totalling 249 goals.
- McCoist also scored eight goals for Sunderland, totalling 290 goals.
- McFadyen also scored 18 goals for Huddersfield Town, totalling 278. In 1939 he joined Clapton Orient, but due to the outbreak of World War Two, his three League appearances (no goals) were expunged from the record books.
- Jimmy McColl scored five goals for Stoke City, plus an unknown number of goals for Leith Athletic after 1931.
- Gordon Wallace scored one goal for Toronto Metros.
- Andy Cunningham scored two goals for Newcastle.
- David McLean scored 162 goals in the English League as follows: Preston 25 goals, Sheffield Wednesday 88 goals and Bradford Park Avenue 49 goals.
- The Scottish totals for Ferguson, Reid, Ferrier, McColl, McLean and Cunningham include goals scored in the Scottish League between 1914 and 1919, which were recognised in Scotland as official seasons.

Chapter 16

Miscellany of facts and figures

This chapter is a compilation of facts and figures that give an insight into Tommy Johnston's career.

• Tommy's first five senior career goals were scored for Peebles Rovers of the Eastern Scottish League in their two Scottish qualifying cup ties against Babcock & Wilcox. Two goals came in a 2–1 win and the other three against the Duns club, in a 3–2 victory, in September 1948. This was followed up in the following season when he scored two hat-tricks against East Stirlingshire during the 1949–50 season. The first match was drawn away 3–3 and they lost the replay at home by 3–4. This led to him being recommended to Kilmarnock by an East Stirlingshire player.

• He was the top goalscorer for Kilmarnock with 15 senior goals in 1949–50, his first season in senior League football.

• He scored on his home League debut for Darlington on 22 August 1951 in a Division Three North fixture against Rochdale, a 2–1 win. This was his first goal in English League football.

- During his spell with Darlington in 1951–52, Tommy scored nine goals for the north-east team, including scoring in four consecutive games.

- Tommy moved to Oldham Athletic in March 1952, scoring twice against Mansfield Town in the final match of the season.

- In June 1952, he moved to Norwich City and in September netted four goals in an 8–1 win at Shrewsbury Town. The following season, he netted the two goals that knocked Arsenal out of the FA Cup in January 1954 – one of his great achievements. He scored 16 senior goals that season, the lowest total of the following eight years.

- Tommy joined Newport County in September 1954 and scored 28 goals in the season, two for Norwich and 26 for the Welsh side.

- A Newport County supporter reckoned in 1956 that Tommy Johnston was County's best forward in the 10 years after World War Two. The club had had some excellent forwards between 1946 and 1956.

- In October 1955, Tommy hit a great hat-trick against Orient: one with his left foot, one with his right and the third with a header. He joined Orient in February 1956 and scored on debut at Swindon Town with a typical bullet header.

- One little-known aspect of Tommy's character was his sense of fairness. In his very first home match for Orient, who thrashed QPR 7–1, the press gave the scorers as Hartburn 4, Heckman 2 and Johnston 1. However, he pointed out to the club that when he had headed the ball into the net, it had already crossed the line from Heckman's lob. So Heckman was credited with a hat-trick. Colleagues told the local press that it was such a close thing that Johnston could easily have claimed the goal.

- Orient won the Third Division South championship after beating Millwall on 26 April 1956. Tommy scored eight goals from 15 matches and his contribution towards promotion was considerable, including the goal that sealed the title. His contribution towards promotion was considerable.

- The best from Johnston was yet to come. He beat Frank Neary's goalscoring record of 25 goals for Orient in 1948–49 by scoring 27 League goals in 1956–57. He went on to score 19 goals from 10 consecutive League and FA Cup matches between 23 November 1957 and 2 January 1958; not too bad for his two seasons in the higher grade.

- In the 1956–57 season, Tommy's first in the Second Division, he scored against all the teams in that division, except for three: Bristol Rovers, Lincoln City and Liverpool.

- The 1957–58 season proved to be his greatest ever. He broke his own goalscoring record of 27 League goals by Christmas Day 1957, when he netted his second goal (he scored four that day) in a 6–2 win over Rotherham United at Brisbane Road.

- After scoring 36 goals for Orient (35 in League and one in the FA Cup) he moved to Blackburn Rovers at the beginning of March 1958 for £15,000 and helped them to promotion to Division One, ending as the top goalscorer in the League in all four divisions.

- He ended the 1957–58 season as the leading goalscorer in the country on 43 League goals with both Orient and Blackburn Rovers. Next came Middlesbrough's Brian Clough on 40. The two were then followed by Bobby Smith of Spurs on 36, Alf Ackerman of Carlisle United on 35, then Bobby Thompson of Preston North End on 34.

Leading League scorers in each Division at the close of the 1957–58 season:

First Division:	36 – Bobby Smith (Spurs); 34 – Tommy Thompson (Preston North End); 33 – Gordon Turner (Luton); 30 – James Murray (Wolves).
Second Division:	43 – **Tommy Johnston** (Leyton Orient and Blackburn Rovers); 40 – Brian Clough (Middlesbrough); 28 – Johnny Summers (Charlton Athletic); 26 – Ron Rafferty (Grimsby Town).
Division Three South:	30 – Derek Reeves (Southampton); 26 – Wilf Carter (Plymouth); 26 – Sam McCrory (Southend United); 26– Eddie Towers (Brentford).
Division Three North:	35 – Alf Ackerman (Carlisle United); 30 – Keith Williams (Tranmere Rovers); 27 – George Stewart (Accrington Stanley).

Authors' Note: Ron Harbertson of Lincoln City scored 27 goals but 22 of those were scored for Darlington in Division Three North. Tommy Johnston led the lists from October 1957, right up to the end of the season.

• When Johnston first left Orient several players were tried at centre-forward, including Len Julians, Derek Nicholson, Stan Willemse and Peter Carey, but Johnston was a very hard act to follow. The following season others were tried: Eddie Lewis, Syd McClellan, Paddy Hasty, Peter Burridge and Tony Biggs. The best was probably Len Julians, but he appeared more comfortable at inside-forward. Johnston scored at least 25 League and FA Cup goals each season from 1954–55 to 1959–60 and his seasonal totals were 28, 29, 27, 44, 25 and 25. He was the only player in the Football League (all Divisions) to achieve this over that six-year period, although two players got close, missing the magic 25 in just one of the seasons concerned. They were John Atyeo (Bristol City) and George Stewart

(Accrington Stanley and Coventry City). Johnston achieved this feat despite being with Norwich City, Newport County, Leyton Orient, Blackburn Rovers and Orient again during those six seasons. Very few players have managed to score 25 League and Cup goals in any consecutive six seasons. Jimmy Greaves is another of those who has.

• Tommy Johnston got off the mark quickly at the start of most seasons. He was a leading divisional goalscorer after the first couple of months of a season.

Tommy Johnston has held Orient's League goalscoring seasonal record for 47 years (at the time of publication in 2004). This is the list of players who have held that League goalscoring record since the O's first League match as members of the Football League back on 2 September 1905 at Leicester Fosse.

Player	Record Broken	Goals	Years held
Walter Leigh	1905–06	8	1905 to 1906
William Martin	1906–07	17	1906 to 1911
Richard McFadden	1911–12	19	1911 to 1914
Richard McFadden	1914–15	21	1914 to 1935
Edmund Crawford	1935–36	23	1935 to 1948
Frank Neary	1948–49	25	1948 to 1956
Tommy Johnston	1956–57	27	1956 to 1957
Tommy Johnston	1957–58	35	1957 to date

Authors' Note: McFadden and Johnston (both Scotsmen) surpassed their own record. Some annuals and publications state that Charlie Fletcher scored 21 goals in the 1931–32 season, which would have equalled McFadden's 1914–15 total, but research has revealed that Fletcher actually scored 20 goals that season.

Only 10 different players have scored 20 or more League goals in a season for Orient since its League entry in the 1905–06 season. Tommy Johnston is the only player to achieve this feat more than once. Johnston is also the only player on the list **not** to complete a full season: that was in the 1957–58 campaign. The full list is:

Player	Season	Goals	Division
Richard McFadden	1914–15	21	2
Charlie Fletcher	1931–32	20	3S
Edmund Crawford	1935–36	23	3S
Frank Neary	1948–49	25	3S
Ken Facey	1954–55	22	3S
Ronnie Heckman	1955–56	23	3S
Johnny Hartburn	1955–56	20	3S
Tommy Johnston	1956–57	27	2
Tommy Johnston	1957–58	35	2
Tommy Johnston	1959–60	25	2
David Dunmore	1961–62	22	2
Peter Kitchen	1977–78	21	2

• Tommy was strong and able to take hard knocks. Despite all the physical attention he received from opponents, he was seldom injured throughout his playing career, and he missed just four League games for Orient during his two spells with the club.

• A remarkable and revealing statistic is that Johnston made a total of 90 away League appearances for Orient and in those matches he scored a total of 52 goals.

• He was sent off three times during his career of 464 senior matches. The first was with Kilmarnock against Dumbarton on 4 March 1950, and he was suspended for one week. The second came on 15 September 1956 for Orient against Doncaster Rovers. O's management pushed for a personal hearing with the FA and, with the help of an outside witness, the FA took the very unusual step of not supporting the referee's decision and cleared Tommy of deliberately attempting to kick an opponent. The third sending off was against Scunthorpe United on 12 December 1959, for retaliating after a succession of niggling fouls (kicks) by the very experienced defenders Jack Brownsword and Brian Heward.

Tommy kicked out at Brownsword and was suspended for one week.

• Tommy made a total of 180 League appearances for Orient and scored 121 goals. That is a tremendous record. If he had scored one every other match, he would have scored 90 goals, but his goals-per-game ratio is far better than that – in fact 31 goals better. However, perhaps the most telling feature of his goalscoring ability is seen when you break those 180 appearances into groups of 10 in the order played. If you look at the goals he netted in each consecutive run of 10 matches it gives you an idea of his consistency. The chart below sets this out:

Tommy Johnston's goalscoring record (League) for Leyton Orient in groups of 10 consecutive matches

Matches	Group	Goals
1 to 10	1	7
11 to 20	2	2
21 to 30	3	7
31 to 40	4	9
41 to 50	5	7
51 to 60	6	5
61 to 70	7	12
71 to 80	8	16
81 to 90	9	8
91 to 100	10	8
101 to 110	11	8
111 to 120	12	7
121 to 130	13	4
131 to 140	14	5
141 to 150	15	7
151 to 160	16	5
161 to 170	17	1
171 to 180	18	3
Totals	180	121

Authors' Note: What can be seen from this chart is that only in groups 2, 17 and possibly 18 was Tommy Johnston not really rattling in the goals. Group 2 was the final part of the 1955–56 season and the early stages of 1956–57 – O's return to its Division Two campaign. Group 17 was the middle part of the 1960–61 season – his final season for the O's when he often played a bit deeper. It is quite incredible that in 11 of these groups, Tommy Johnston scored seven or more goals, and in Group 8 he notched 16; that was during his record-breaking 1957–58 campaign.

- Tommy's 200th League career goal was scored at Liverpool on 21 November 1959 while with Orient. His 100th League goal for the O's came at Sunderland on 20 February 1960.

- He holds Orient's record in scoring in consecutive matches, scoring 10 times (nine in the League and once in the FA Cup). David Halliday scored in nine consecutive League games in the 1933–34 season.

- During Tommy's Orient career, he had quite a number of goals disallowed. Ten goals were disallowed in his record-breaking season of 1957–58, of which three were extremely dubious decisions: against Liverpool (home), Grimsby Town (away) and Fulham (away). His total for that season should have been higher.

- His career record in senior Cup matches was as follows: 12 Scottish Cup matches, 18 goals. He played in three Welsh Cup matches and scored six goals. He made 19 appearances in the FA Cup and netted nine goals and finally he played in three Football League Cup games without scoring.

- When one considers that Tommy Johnston scored 290 senior career goals, it is amazing that he only converted six penalties. No records are available on the number, if any, he missed for his other clubs. He missed two spot-kicks for Orient versus Liverpool on 21 September 1957 and versus Notts County on 23 November 1957.

The converted spot-kicks were:

Newport County v Queens Park Rangers	H	22 January 1955
Newport County v Swindon Town	H	8 April 1955
Newport County v Brentford	H	21 April 1955
Newport County v Leyton Orient	H	30 April 1955
Leyton Orient v Cardiff City	H	14 September 1957
Leyton Orient v Barnsley	H	12 October 1957

• During Tommy's career he scored four goals twice and nabbed 11 hat-tricks in League and senior Cup matches. These were as follows:

Four goals

Norwich City	v Shrewsbury Town	Div 3 South	A	13 September 1952
Leyton Orient	v Rotherham United	Div 2	H	25 December 1957

Three goals

Peebles Rovers	v Coldstream	Scottish Cup	A	September 1947
Peebles Rovers	v Duns	Scottish Cup	H	September 1948
Peebles Rovers	v East Stirlingshire	ScottishCup	A	10 September 1949
Peebles Rovers	v East Stirlingshire	Scottish Cup (R)	H	14 September 1949
Newport County	v Leyton Orient	Div 3 South	H	8 October 1955
Newport County	v Barry Town	Welsh Cup	H	28 January 1956
Leyton Orient	v Aldershot	Div 3 South	H	17 March 1956
Leyton Orient	v Swansea Town	Div 2	H	26 October 1957
Leyton Orient	v Grimsby Town	Div 2	H	21 December 1957
Leyton Orient	v Bristol City	Div 2	H	11 January 1958
Blackburn Rovers	v Newcastle United	Div 1	H	20 December 1958

• Of the 186 matches Johnston could have played for the O's during his two spells, he actually made 180 appearances. He was absent for just six matches, four through injury and two after being dropped to give young striker Alan Sealey a run.

• Tommy's last goal for Orient in League football was a vital shot. It meant that Orient retained their Second Division status over Norwich City in April 1961. His final League appearance came at Lincoln City later that month.

• Johnston was not one for making a fuss when he scored his goals. Whenever he scored from a cross, he would just run over to that player, shake his hand and then run back to the centre circle to restart the game. It was the Continental players who brought the dramatics into the game. Players in his day were less demonstrative and most of the players at Leyton Orient were the same, except for Eddie Brown and later Mark Lazarus who would go running around the ground like greyhounds and were most outgoing in their celebrations.

• Over the years, Johnston recommended a few players to Orient: Billy Taylor from Bonnyrigg Rose in Scotland during 1959; Billy Rennie from Loanhead Mayflower in 1960; and Gordon Butler from Lytham St Annes in 1965. Only Taylor went on to play in the first team for the O's.

• Tommy's final career League goal was scored in Division Four for Gillingham in a 2–2 draw on 14 April 1962. Ironically their opponents that day were Darlington, his first English club. The goal was his 290th senior career goal from 464 appearances.

Leyton Orient records held by Tommy Johnston

Aggregate goalscoring record: 121 goals.

Seasonal goalscoring record: 35 goals.

Only player to top goalscoring charts: 44 goals (eight goals for Blackburn Rovers) 1957–58 – 36 for Orient.

Most hat-tricks in League: five (including one four-goal haul).

Only player to score hat-tricks in consecutive matches: 3 v Grimsby Town (h) 21 Dec 1957; and 4 v Rotherham United (h) 25 Dec 1957.

Longest run of consecutive League matches scoring a goal: nine in 1957–58, held jointly with David Halliday.

Longest run of consecutive senior games scoring a goal: 10 in 1957–58.

Only player to score than 100 League goals for the club.

Only player to create a new club League goalscoring record, then beat it in the following season.

Most seasons as top League goalscorer: five (one season joint-top).

Only player to score more than 20 League goals in a season more than once: three times in 1956–57, 1957–58 and 1959–60.

Only one of 10 players to score four goals in a League game: v Rotherham United (h) 25 December 1957.

Most League goals scored on away grounds: 52 from 90 matches.

Scored two goals in a League match more than any other player: 23 times.

Tommy Johnston's career with Leyton Orient: appearance and goalscoring record

Season	Division	League		FA Cup		FL Cup		Total	
		Apps	Gls	Apps	Gls	Apps	Gls	Apps	Gls
1955–56	3S	15	8	0	0	-	-	15	8
1956–57	2	42	27	1	0	-	-	43	27
1957–58	2	30	35*	2	1	-	-	32	36
1958–59	2	14	10	0	0	-	-	14	10
1959–60	2	39	25	1	0	-	-	40	25
1960–61+	2	40	16	3	1	3	0	46	17
		180	121	7	2	3	0	190	123

* Club record

+ First season of the FL Cup

Authors' Note: The above list does not include any minor cup, tour or friendly matches.

Promotion is clinched for Blackburn at Charlton.

Liverpool goalkeeper Tommy Younger, a great friend of Johnston's, catches the ball under pressure from Leyton Orient's Tommy Johnston on 28 February 1959, the third game back at Brisbane Road since Tommy's return from Blackburn. Liverpool ran out winners 3-1.

Tommy scores against Sunderland in O's great 6–1 win in March 1959.

Les Gore congratulates Eddie Brown after scoring his 200th League goal against Middlesbrough in the last game of the 1959–60 season. Tommy Johnston, who scored his 200th League goal against Liverpool a few weeks earlier, looks on.

Leyton Orient 1960–61. Back row: S. Charlton, K. Facey, S. Bishop, F. George, C. Lea, E. Lewis. Front row: E. Crossan, J. Elwood, T. Johnston, D. Gibbs, R. Newman.

Gillingham in 1961–62. Tommy is in the centre of the front row.

The leaving presentation to Tommy at the Folkestone supporters club in 1964.

Outside the Tommy Johnston bar at Brisbane Road. From left to right: long-standing O's supporter Sid Barrett, LOSC committee member Lou Day, Sid Bishop, LOSC deputy chairman Steve Jenkins, Stan Charlton, Keith Francis and LOSC chairman and a director of LOFC David Dodd.

Tommy in Australia in 1989.

Tommy with the founder members of the O's supporters' club in Australia, Phil and Brian Timms, outside the Johnstons' house in Sanctuary Point, New South Wales.

Leyton Orient legend Tommy Johnston presents Steve Castle with the *Hackney Gazette* player-of-the-month award in September 1989.

One of the tankards in this picture was presented to Tommy by Leyton Orient in 1957, for his 36 goals. The other was sent to him on his 70th birthday by O's supporter Martin P. Smith, along with a birthday card from Leyton Orient Football Club.

Jean and Tommy as they are today, in Australia.

Tommy Johnston with his sporting medals and trophies, photographed for this book in 2004.

Chapter 17

In conclusion – the authors write

At the moment, the name of Tommy Johnston is unlikely to be included in most football fans' lists of their top players of all time. But wherever you place him in your list it seems fairly certain that he should be a great deal higher-placed than he is generally is. There were lots of talented forwards around in the 1950s but none, in the view of the authors, ever looked so downright menacing to the opposition in the air as Tommy Johnston. He looked a class player in all the Divisions he played in and he was the best of them all in his heading ability. He scored a total of 290 career senior goals from 464 appearances.

Throughout this book we have tried to show the extent of Tommy Johnston's talents, and in particular his genius at heading – perhaps to say 'he simply was the best' is enough. Bigger and better clubs have had all manner of great players over the years, but we don't think there has ever been a better header of the ball than Tommy Johnston.

Another fact is that Tommy Johnston is ranked joint-53rd in the list of the all-time top goalscorers in the English League, and joint 19th in the list of the all-time leading League goalscorers by season. When one considers that there have been approximately 38,000 players to have made an appearance in the Football League between 1888 and January 2004 – of which almost 8,000 were forwards – his achievements seem remarkable.

There might be a temptation, when writing a book about a player, to stress the positive aspects of their play, life and career and overlook the negative. However, in compiling this book the authors looked through their extensive library of football records and articles, match reports and all the rest, and they genuinely found very little that could be construed as critical or negative. Nearly all the general remarks made about him in the press said just how brilliant he was, and there were just two instances among hundreds of articles where anything less than unreserved praise was given. One related to him playing for Orient at Cardiff City in the FA Cup on 25 January 1959 while carrying an injury throughout the match, while the other was made when he was playing for Folkestone Town in the Southern League after recovering from a serious car accident in 1962.

Tommy Johnston was a good honest professional, who took hard knocks without complaint and epitomised the give-and-take approach and the correct attitude. He was under-rated, even though people inside the game spoke very highly of his ability, and sadly the Scottish selectors of his time misjudged his worth.

Above all, he was a genius at heading a football. Genius is an oft-misused word – but in this instance it is the only word that fits.

Perhaps Tommy's experience down the mine helped to shape his attitude to the game. We reckon he realised that footballers were fortunate to be paid for what they did, although in those days they were certainly not paid excessively – far from it.

He was a credit to his profession and a great player. We would like to thank him for some of the very best Orient performances ever witnessed.

Neilson N. Kaufman and Alan E. Ravenhill
2004

Epilogue

The last word – by Tommy Johnston

The last word should belong to the man himself. Tommy Johnston says:

Trophies and honours have not been plentiful for me. Everyone likes winning things and representing their country of birth, but the game is more important to me. As a working-class man, I just loved playing football, especially for Leyton Orient.

A couple of great highlights in my career were most certainly winning medals in the promotion seasons with Leyton Orient in 1956 and then Blackburn Rovers in 1958. I also received a cigarette lighter from the Sporting Record *for my goals in the Norwich Cup tie at Arsenal, and an 'Andy Cap' from the* Daily Mirror *when with Blackburn. That's as far as it went as regards my awards in football. There are my three wonderful tankards – two from Leyton Orient and one from Folkestone Town –*

which still, to this day, hold pride of place on my sideboard. I also won a few trophies for snooker in Australia.

They say that a rolling stone gathers no moss. I certainly haven't gathered much, but I thoroughly enjoyed my years in football as the 'Happy Wanderer'. I was also called 'The man with the magic feet'. I wouldn't have missed it for the world.

I hope this book inspires young people to never give up on their dreams, no matter what life may bring you along the way.

With Best Wishes

Tommy Johnston.

Tommy Johnston
Sanctuary Point, New South Wales
Australia
2004

Authors' Note: Tommy's open-heart surgery in September 2004

After a variety of tests in mid-2004 and an angiogram on 5 July, Tommy was told that he needed open-heart surgery to correct a problem with his mitral valve and aorta. He was asked to go away and consider his options.

A month or so later Tommy decided to go ahead with the operation and a date was fixed for Setpember 2004. On 19 July he and Jean couple celebrated 52 years of marriage and thereafter made plans for the risky operation.

Jean saw that Tommy had aged over the past six months; in hindsight it was obviously down to the heart problem. Also his short-term memory loss was very noticable. However, when it came to football, he remembered everything.

The family gave permission for the news to be released to the various Leyton Orient related websites and were amazed by the number mumber of get-well messages they received by email and through the post. They could not believe that after more than 40 years both old and new fans still fondly remembered him.

The time arrived for the operation and on 7 September Jean and Tommy travelled to the Prince of Wales Hospital in Randwick, Sydney for the next day's operation.

The surgery was performed by Dr Con Manganas and his team of seven other doctors (one young doctor, Ben Smith, was from Oxford, England). The operation turned out to be a great success and Tommy has recovered well, with just a niggling problem with a leg wound where they took a vein out for use in the heart. Tommy was in hospital for a week and is now recuperating fully at home.

We print below just a few extracts from the many messages received by Orient fans:

Martin Smith wrote that at the O's home match on 11 September an annoucment was made over the loudspeaker before kick-off about Tommy's recovery and a great cheer went up. It inspired the team to one of their best wins for quite a while, 4–2 over Bristol Rovers.

Barry Corbett's email stated: I am 40 years old and went to my first Leyton Orient match in 1972 when I was eight.

My parents put me on the right path in following the O's. Sadly they have both passed on now, but they constantly spoke about you Tommy. You clearly held a very special place in their hearts for the entertainment that you provided. Hardly a match would go by without one of them reminding me about just how brilliant a player you were, truly the finest ever to grace the turf at Brisbane Road. Even in their later years if football was on the telly and an absolute sitter was missed they would say 'Tommy Johnston would have netted that'. My Dad's other saying was 'Tommy Johnston even if he had a bloody boot on his head, he wouldn't miss chances'.

I would have dearly have loved to see you play, as over the years many elder statesmen have spoken about you similarly in such high regard.

I hope that this hasn't bored you but to a die-hard O's fella like myself, you were the greatest at the club that I love.

A flash in the pan has his day… but legends live on forever. Sincere best wishes that you overcome your illness mate.

Aidan Taylor emailed: As an Orient fan, and a nurse on a coronary care ward, I wish you all the very best on your decisions and on your future health. You truly are a legend amongst O's fans, known and remembered by all, young and old, and we wish you all the best at this difficult time in your life.

John Wallace wrote: Having been an O's supporter since my Dad took me to Brisbane Road as a nipper in the early 1950s, I can clearly remember those good old days when you were knocking the ball in the net for us (and your famous spell with Blackburn Rovers). Last night I read an article in the *London Evening Standard* that you are having a heart operation and I cannot but wish you well and let you know you are in my thoughts. Please accept my best wishes for a speedy recovery Tommy.

Appendix

Full career appearance and goalscoring record, 1947–62

There follows a full record of Tommy Johnston's professional career with all his clubs. FA Cup details are shown as (FAC), Football League Cup as (FLC), Scottish Qualifying Cup as (SQC), Scottish League Cup as (SLC), 'B' Division Supplementary Cup as (BDSC), Welsh Cup as (WC) and minor cup and other known matches are shown after each of the club's listings.

Peebles Rovers
Peebles Rovers were a juvenile team that played in the Eastern Scottish League. Records of these matches are not available, and they would not normally be included because they are juvenile matches. However, Tommy Johnston played in six Scottish Qualifying Cup ties for them between 1947 and 1949, scoring a remarkable 15 goals. These previously unknown statistics have now been added to Johnston's career totals.

Opposition	Venue	Score	Goals Scored	Date (if known)
Peebles Rovers 1947–48 Scottish Qualifying Cup (south)				
Coldstream	A	5–0	3	Sept (SQC) 1st Round
Edinburgh City	A	1–7	1	Sept (SQC) 2nd Round
Peebles Rovers 1948–49 Scottish Qualifying Cup (south)				
Babcock & Wilcox	H	2–1	2	Sept (SQC) 1st Round
Duns	H	3–2	3	Sept (SQC) 2nd Round
Peebles Rovers 1949–50 Scottish Qualifying Cup (south)				
East Stirlingshire	A	3–3	3	10 Sept (SQC) 1st Round
East Stirlingshire	H	3–4	3	14 Sept (SQC) 1st Round Replay
Kilmarnock Scottish League 'B' Division 1949–50				
Hamilton Academical	H	2–0	2	10 Dec
Alloa Athletic	A	3–2	2	17 Dec
Albion Rovers	H	2–1	1	24 Dec
Arbroath	A	2–1	2	31 Dec
Ayr United	H	4–0	1	2 Jan
Dundee United	A	0–3	-	3 Jan
Morton	H	2–0	-	7 Jan
Queens Park	A	3–1	1	14 Jan
Forfar Athletic	H	0–1	-	21 Jan
Stirling Albion	H	1–1	1	28 Jan (SFAC 1st Round)
Stirling Albion	A	1–3	-	1 Feb (SFAC Replay)
Dunfermline Athletic	H	3–2	2	4 Feb
Stenhousemuir	H	3–2	1	18 Feb
Airdrieonians	A	0–2	-	25 Feb
Dumbarton (sent off)	H	1–1	1	4 March
St Johnstone	H	1–1	-	11 March
Airdrieonians	H	2–1	-	25 April (BDSP)
St Johnstone	A	2–2	1	10 May (BDSP) Semi-final

Opposition	Venue	Score	Goals Scored	Date (if known)
Friendlies				
Buckie Thistle	H	2–1	1	8 April
Derby County	H	1–5	-	19 April
Derry City	H	10–3	5	22 April
Peebles Rovers	A	1–1	-	3 May

Kilmarnock Scottish League 'B' Division 1950–51

Opposition	Venue	Score	Goals Scored	Date (if known)
Dunfermline Athletic	H	3–1	1	12 Aug (SLC Qual Section)
Ayr United	A	2–2	-	16 Aug
Dumbarton	A	0–1	-	19 Aug
Arbroath	A	2–0	1	16 Sept
Alloa Athletic	H	2–2	1	11 Nov
Queens Park	H	3–4	1	13 Jan
East Stirlingshire	A	1–2	-	27 Jan (SFAC, 1st Round)
Dunfermline Athletic	A	2–4	1	3 Feb

Darlington Division Three North 1951–52

Opposition	Venue	Score	Goals Scored	Date (if known)
Crewe Alexandra	A	0–3	-	18 Aug
Rochdale	H	2–1	1	22 Aug
Southport	H	1–1	-	25 Aug
Rochdale	A	2–6	-	28Aug
Tranmere Rovers	A	0–3	-	1 Sept
Oldham Athletic	H	2–2	-	5 Sept
Scunthorpe United	H	2–3	1	8 Sept
Oldham Athletic	A	2–3	1	11 Sept
Lincoln City	A	2–7	1	15 Sept
Hartlepools United	H	2–1	1	19 Sept
Chester	H	1–1	1	22 Sept
York City	A	1–2	-	29 Sept
Carlisle United	A	1–1	-	6 Oct
Stockport County	H	1–2	-	13 Oct
Workington	A	1–2	-	20 Oct
Barrow	H	1–2	-	22 Oct
Grimsby Town	A	0–3	-	3 Nov

Opposition	Venue	Score	Goals Scored	Date (if known)
Mansfield Town	H	2–1	1	8 Dec
Crewe Alexandra	H	0–1	-	15 Dec
Southport	A	0–3	-	22 Dec
Accrington Stanley	H	4–5	-	25 Dec
Accrington Stanley	A	3–1	-	26 Dec
Tranmere Rovers	H	2–1	1	29 Dec
Scunthorpe United	A	2–5	1	5 Jan
Lincoln City	H	1–1	-	19 Jan
Gateshead	A	2–2	1	23 Jan
York City	H	1–0	-	9 Feb

Oldham Athletic Division Three North 1951–52

Opposition	Venue	Score	Goals Scored	Date (if known)
Carlisle United	A	3–3	-	1 March
Stockport County	H	1–0	1	8 March
Workington	A	1–0	-	15 March
Grimsby Town	A	1–3	-	29 March
Mansfield Town	H	5–3	2	3 May

Norwich City Division Three South 1952–53

Opposition	Venue	Score	Goals Scored	Date (if known)
Aldershot	H	5–0	1	23 Aug
Ipswich Town	A	1–2	-	27 Aug
Swindon Town	A	1–2	1	30 Aug
Ipswich Town	H	1–0	1	3 Sept
Queens Park Rangers	H	2–0	1	6 Sept
Exeter City	A	0–1	-	10 Sept
Shrewsbury Town	A	8–1	4	13 Sept
Exeter City	H	2–0	1	17 Sept
Walsall	H	3–0	1	20 Sept
Crystal Palace	A	1–1	-	24 Sept
Bournemouth	H	1–1	1	18 Oct
Southend United	A	2–1	-	25 Oct
Watford	H	5–2	-	1 Nov
Brighton & Hove Alb	A	3–2	-	8 Nov
Newport County	H	2–0	1	15 Nov

Opposition	Venue	Score	Goals Scored	Date (if known)
Tonbridge	A	2–2	-	22 Nov (FAC)
Tonbridge	H	1–0	-	27 Nov (FAC Replay)
Bristol City	H	0–0	-	29 Nov
Brighton & Hove Alb	A	0–2	-	6 Dec (FAC)
Northampton Town	H	1–2	1	13 Dec
Aldershot	A	2–1	-	20 Dec
Queens Park Rangers	A	1–3	-	17 Jan
Walsall	A	2–3	-	29 Jan
Newport County	A	1–1	-	4 April
Torquay United	H	3–0	1	25 April
Northampton Town	A	3–3	1	30 April
Colchester United	A	4–0	-	2 May

Norwich City Division Three South 1953–54

Opposition	Venue	Score	Goals Scored	Date (if known)
Southend United	H	1–0	-	19 Aug
Aldershot	A	0–0	-	22 Aug
Queens Park Rangers	A	2–0	1	31 Aug
Walsall	A	4–1	1	5 Sept
Colchester United	H	2–1	-	9 Sept
Shrewsbury Town	H	1–0	1	12 Sept
Southend United	A	2–5	-	31 Oct
Bournemouth	H	1–3	-	5 Dec
Barnsley	H	2–1	2	12 Dec (FAC)
Aldershot	H	3–3	-	19 Dec
Crystal Palace	A	0–1	-	25 Dec
Crystal Palace	H	2–1	1	26 Dec
Swindon Town	A	0–0	-	2 Jan
Hastings	H	3–0	1	13 Jan (FAC)
Walsall	H	3–0	1	16 Jan
Shrewsbury Town	A	0–4	-	23 Jan
Arsenal	A	2–1	2	30 Jan (FAC)
Exeter City	H	1–2	-	6 Feb
Newport County	A	1–4	-	13 Feb
Leicester City	H	1–2	-	20Feb (FAC)

Opposition	Venue	Score	Goals Scored	Date (if known)
Gillingham	H	0–0	-	24 Feb
Torquay United	A	4–2	-	27 Feb
Watford	H	4–1	1	6 March
Millwall	A	3–1	-	13 March
Southampton	A	0–0	-	24 March
Reading	A	4–4	2	27 March
Leyton Orient	H	3–1	2	3 April
Bournemouth	A	0–2	-	10 April
Coventry City	H	2–1	-	17 April
Brighton & Hove Alb	A	0–0	-	24 April
Coventry City	A	0–1	-	26 April
Millwall	H	4–3	1	28 April
Southampton	H	1–0	-	1 May

Norwich City Third Division South 1954–55

Opposition	Venue	Score	Goals Scored	Date (if known)
Aldershot	H	4–3	-	21 Aug
Crystal Palace	H	2–0	-	4 Sept
Exeter City	A	1–0	-	8 Sept
Northampton Town	A	1–1	-	11 Sept
Exeter City	H	3–0	2	15 Sept
Watford	H	3–1	-	18 Sept
Colchester United	A	0–1	-	23 Sept

Newport County Third Division South 1954–55

Opposition	Venue	Score	Goals Scored	Date (if known)
Southampton	A	0–2	-	16 Oct
Millwall	H	2–1	-	23 Oct
Torquay United	A	3–2	2	30 Oct
Gillingham	H	1–3	-	6 Nov
Reading	A	1–2	1	13 Nov
Gillingham	A	0–2	-	20 Nov (FAC)
Walsall	A	3–3	2	27 Nov
Bristol City	H	2–2	2	4 Dec
Northampton Town	A	2–2	-	18 Dec
Crystal Palace	A	1–2	1	25 Dec

Opposition	Venue	Score	Goals Scored	Date (if known)
Crystal Palace	H	0–1	-	27 Dec
Watford	H	0–0	-	1 Jan
Abergavenny	H	6–0	2	13 Jan (Welsh Cup)
Bournemouth	A	3–3	1	15 Jan
Queens Park Rangers	H	4–0	2 (1pen)	22 Jan
Brighton & Hove Alb	H	1–3	-	5 Feb
Exeter City	A	1–1	1	12 Feb
Cardiff City	H	1–3	1	17 Feb (Welsh Cup)
Colchester United	H	0–0	-	19 Feb
Southampton	H	0–1	-	5 March
Millwall	A	1–1	1	12 March
Leyton Orient	A	2–1	1	17 March
Torquay United	H	1–1	1	19 March
Gillingham	A	2–4	2	26 March
Reading	H	3–1	2	2 April
Coventry City	A	2–3	1	4 April
Swindon Town	H	2–2	1 (pen)	8 April
Shrewsbury Town	A	0–3	-	9 April
Swindon Town	A	3–1	1	11 April
Walsall	H	1–0	-	16 April
Brentford	H	3–1	2 (1 pen)	21 April
Bristol City	A	0–0	-	23 April
Shrewsbury Town	H	1–1	1	28 April
Leyton Orient	H	1–2	1 (pen)	30 April
Brentford	A	0–1	-	2 May

Newport County 1955–56 Division Three South

Opposition	Venue	Score	Goals Scored	Date (if known)
Shrewsbury Town	A	0–5	-	20 Aug
Aldershot	A	0–1	-	24 Aug
Ipswich Town	H	2–1	-	27 Aug
Aldershot	H	0–1	-	1 Sept
Walsall	A	3–3	2	3 Sept
Southampton	H	1–0	-	8 Sept
Torquay United	H	2–1	-	10 Sept

Opposition	Venue	Score	Goals Scored	Date (if known)
Southampton	A	3–3	1	14 Sept
Southend United	A	1–4	1	17 Sept
Crystal Palace	H	0–1	-	22 Sept
Swindon Town	A	2–1	1	24 Sept
Northampton Town	H	0–1	-	29 Sept
Queens Park Rangers	H	2–1	-	1 Oct
Leyton Orient	H	3–0	3	8 Oct
Colchester United	A	1–2	1	15 Oct
Norwich City	H	2–2	1	22 Oct
Bournemouth	A	0–0	-	29 Oct
Gillingham	H	3–2	2	5 Nov
Millwall	A	4–2	1	12 Nov
Brighton & Hove Alb	A	1–8	1	19 Nov (FAC)
Watford	A	1–1	1	26 Nov
Brentford	H	1–2	-	3 Dec
Coventry City	A	0–3	-	10 Dec.
Shrewsbury Town	H	1–2	-	17 Dec
Ipswich Town	A	2–3	2	24 Dec
Brighton & Hove Alb	A	1–4	1	26 Dec
Brighton & Hove Alb	H	1–0	1	27 Dec
Walsall	H	2–0	-	31 Dec
Reading	H	2–3	-	7 Jan
Torquay United	A	1–1	1	14 Jan
Barry Town	H	8–1	3	28 Jan (Welsh Cup)
Queens Park Rangers	A	0–0	-	11 Feb
Leyton Orient	A	1–3	1	13 Feb

Leyton Orient Division Three South 1955–56

Swindon Town	A	2–1	1	25 Feb
Queens Park Rangers	H	7–1	-	3 March
Northampton Town	A	1–0	-	10 March
Aldershot	H	8–3	3	17 March
Crystal Palace	A	2–1	1	24 March
Torquay United	H	3–2	-	30 March

Opposition	Venue	Score	Goals Scored	Date (if known)
Brighton & Hove Alb	H	0–1	-	31 March
Torquay United	A	3–1	-	2 April
Southampton	A	2–1	-	7 April
Shrewsbury Town	H	5–2	2	14 April
Brighton & Hove Alb	A	1–1	-	18 April
Ipswich Town	A	0–2	-	21 April
Millwall	H	2–1	1	26 April
Millwall	A	0–5	-	30 April
Ipswich Town	H	1–2	-	3 May

Leyton Orient 1956–57 Division Two

Opposition	Venue	Score	Goals Scored	Date (if known)
Nottingham Forest	H	1–4	-	18 Aug
Bristol Rovers	H	1–1	-	23 Aug
Huddersfield Town	A	0–3	-	25 Aug
Bristol Rovers	A	2–3	-	27 Aug
Bury	H	4–3	1	1 Sept
Grimsby Town	A	0–0	-	8 Sept
Notts County	A	3–1	1	13 Sept
Doncaster R (sent off)	H	1–1	-	15 Sept
Stoke City	A	1–7	1	22 Sept
Middlesbrough	H	1–1	-	29 Sept
West Ham United	H	1–2	-	6 Oct
Blackburn Rovers	A	3–3	1	13 Oct
Swansea Town	H	3–0	1	20 Oct
Sheffield United	A	3–2	1	27 Oct
Barnsley	H	2–0	2	3 Nov
Port Vale	A	2–1	1	10 Nov
Rotherham United	H	2–1	1	17 Nov
Lincoln City	A	2–0	-	24 Nov
Bristol City	H	2–2	1	1 Dec
Fulham	A	1–3	1	8 Dec
Nottingham Forest	A	2–1	2	15 Dec
Huddersfield Town	H	3–1	1	22 Dec
Liverpool	A	0–1	-	25 Dec

Opposition	Venue	Score	Goals Scored	Date (if known)
Liverpool	H	0–4	-	26 Dec
Bury	A	3–1	2	29 Dec
Chelsea	H	0–2	-	5 Jan (FAC)
Grimsby Town	H	1–1	1	12 Jan
Doncaster Rovers	A	1–6	1	19 Jan
Stoke City	H	2–2	2	2 Feb
Middlesbrough	A	2–1	1	9 Feb
West Ham United	A	1–2	1	16 Feb
Blackburn Rovers	H	1–1	-	23 Feb
Swansea Town	A	0–1	-	2 March
Sheffield United	H	1–2	-	9 March
Barnsley	A	0–3	-	16 March
Port Vale	H	3–2	1	23 March
Rotherham United	A	0–2	-	30 March
Lincoln City	H	2–1	-	6 April
Bristol City	A	2–4	-	13 April
Leicester City	H	1–5	1	19 April
Fulham	H	0–2	-	20 April
Leicester City	A	4–1	1	22 April
Notts County	H	2–2	1	27 April

Leyton Orient 1957–58 Division Two

Opposition	Venue	Score	Goals Scored	Date (if known)
Grimsby Town	A	2–7	2	24 Aug
Doncaster Rovers	A	0–2	-	28 Aug
Stoke City	H	0–2	-	31 Aug
Doncaster Rovers	H	2–0	2	5 Sept
Bristol City	A	2–2	1	7 Sept
Charlton Athletic	A	2–3	2	12 Sept
Cardiff City	H	4–2	2 (1 pen)	14 Sept
Charlton Athletic	H	3–2	2	19 Sept
Liverpool	A	0–3	-	21 Sept
Middlesbrough	H	4–0	-	28 Sept
West Ham United	A	2–3	1	5 Oct
Barnsley	H	2–1	2 (1 pen)	12 Oct

Opposition	Venue	Score	Goals Scored	Date (if known)
Fulham	A	1–3	-	19 Oct
Swansea Town	H	5–1	3	26 Oct
Derby County	A	0–2	-	2 Nov
Bristol Rovers	H	1–3	-	9 Nov
Lincoln City	A	0–2	-	16 Nov
Notts County	H	2–2	2	23 Nov
Ipswich Town	A	3–5	1	30 Nov
Blackburn Rovers	H	5–1	2	7 Dec
Sheffield United	A	2–0	1	14 Dec
Grimsby Town	H	5–1	3	21 Dec
Rotherham United	H	6–2	4	25 Dec
Rotherham United	A	2–2	1	26 Dec
Stoke City	A	3–1	1	28 Dec
Reading	H	1–0	1	4 Jan (FAC)
Bristol City	H	4–0	3	11 Jan
Cardiff City	A	1–1	-	18 Jan
Cardiff City	A	1–4	-	25 Jan (FAC)
Liverpool	H	1–0	-	1 Feb
West Ham United	A	1–4	-	20 Feb
Notts County	A	1–0	-	22 Feb

Blackburn Rovers 1957–58 Division Two

Opposition	Venue	Score	Goals Scored	Date (if known)
Grimsby Town	H	3–0	2	8 March
Stoke City	A	4–2	1	15 March
Bristol City	H	5–0	-	24 March
Cardiff City	A	3–4	1	29 March
Doncaster Rovers	A	5–1	1	4 April
Rotherham United	H	5–0	2	5 April
Doncaster Rovers	H	3–2	1	7 April
Middlesbrough	A	3–2	-	12 April
Leyton Orient	H	4–1	-	19 April
Fulham	A	1–1	-	23 April
Charlton Athletic	A	4–3	-	26 April

Opposition	Venue	Score	Goals Scored	Date (if known)
Blackburn Rovers 1958–59 Division One				
Newcastle United	A	5–1	2	23 Aug
Leicester City	H	5–0	1	25 Aug
Tottenham Hotspur	H	5–0	2	30 Aug
Leicester City	A	1–1	-	3 Sept
Manchester United	A	1–6	-	6 Sept
Blackpool	A	1–1	-	8 Sept
Wolverhampton Wand	H	1–2	-	13 Sept
Blackpool	H	0–0	-	15 Sept
Portsmouth	A	1–2	1	20 Sept
Aston Villa	H	2–3	2	27 Sept
West Ham United	A	3–6	-	4 Oct
Burnley	A	0–0	-	18 Oct
Arsenal	H	4–2	-	25 Oct
Everton	A	2–2	-	1 Nov
Birmingham City	H	3–2	-	8 Nov
West Bromwich Albion	A	3–2	1	15 Nov
Leeds United	H	2–4	-	22 Nov
Manchester City	A	1–0	1	29 Nov
Bolton Wanderers	H	1–1	-	6 Dec
Luton Town	A	1–1	1	13 Dec
Newcastle United	H	3–0	3	20 Dec
Chelsea	H	0–3	-	25 Dec
Chelsea	A	2–0	-	27 Dec
Tottenham Hotspur	A	1–3	-	3 Jan
Leyton Orient	H	4–2	1	10 Jan (FAC)
Burnley	H	1–2	-	28 Jan (FAC)
Wolverhampton Wand	A	0–5	-	31 Jan
Leyton Orient 1958–59 Division Two				
Fulham	A	2–5	-	14 Feb
Lincoln City	H	0–0	-	21 Feb
Liverpool	H	1–3	-	28 Feb
Sheffield United	A	3–2	2	7 March

Opposition	Venue	Score	Goals Scored	Date (if known)
Brighton & Hove Alb	H	2–2	1	14 March
Huddersfield Town	A	0–0	-	21 Feb
Rotherham United	H	2–0	-	28 March
Sunderland	H	6–0	1	30 March
Middlesbrough	A	2–4	-	4 April
Charlton Athletic	H	6–1	-	11 April
Bristol City	A	1–0	1	18 April
Grimsby Town	A	1–4	1	21 April
Cardiff City	H	3–0	2	25 April
Barnsley	A	3–1	2	29 April

Leyton Orient 1959–60 Division Two

Opposition	Venue	Score	Goals Scored	Date (if known)
Bristol Rovers	A	2–2	1	22 Aug
Stoke City	H	2–1	1	27 Aug
Ipswich Town	H	4–1	2	29 Aug
Stoke City	A	1–2	1	2 Sept
Huddersfield Town	A	1–1	-	5 Sept
Brighton & Hove Alb	H	3–2	1	10 Sept
Rotherham United	H	2–3	2	12 Sept
Brighton & Hove Alb	A	1–1	1	16 Sept
Lincoln City	H	4–1	-	19 Sept
Aston Villa	A	0–1	-	26 Sept
Sunderland	H	1–1	-	3 Oct
Cardiff City	A	1–5	1	10 Oct
Hull City	H	3–1	2	17 Oct
Sheffield United	A	2–0	1	24 Oct
Middlesbrough	H	5–0	1	31 Oct
Derby County	A	1–1	-	7 Nov
Plymouth Argyle	H	2–3	-	14 Nov
Liverpool	A	3–4	2	21 Nov
Charlton Athletic	H	2–0	-	28 Nov
Bristol City	A	1–1	1	5 Dec
Scunthorpe U (sent off)	H	1–1	-	12 Dec
Bristol Rovers	H	1–2	-	19 Dec

Opposition	Venue	Score	Goals Scored	Date (if known)
Portsmouth	H	1–2	-	26 Dec
Portsmouth	A	1–1	-	28 Dec
Ipswich Town	A	3–6	-	2 Jan
Liverpool	A	1–2	-	9 Jan (FAC)
Huddersfield Town	H	2–1	1	16 Jan
Lincoln City	A	2–2	1	6 Feb
Aston Villa	H	0–0	-	13 Feb
Sunderland	H	4–1	1	20 Feb
Cardiff City	H	3–4	2	27 Feb
Hull City	A	2–1	1	5 March
Sheffield United	H	1–1	-	17 March
Plymouth Argyle	A	0–1	-	2 April
Liverpool	H	2–0	1	9 April
Swansea Town	H	2–1	-	15 April
Scunthorpe United	A	1–2	-	16 April
Swansea Town	A	0–1	-	18 April
Bristol City	H	3–1	-	23 April
Middlesbrough	A	2–2	1	30 April

Leyton Orient 1960–61 Division Two

Opposition	Venue	Score	Goals Scored	Date (if known)
Ipswich Town	H	1–3	1	20 Aug
Brighton & Hove Alb	A	1–1	1	24 Aug
Scunthorpe United	A	2–2	2	27 Aug
Brighton & Hove Alb	H	2–1	-	31 Aug
Sheffield United	A	1–4	-	3 Sept
Leeds United	H	3–1	1	7 Sept
Derby County	H	2–1	2	10 Sept
Leeds United	H	0–1	-	14 Sept
Bristol Rovers	A	2–4	-	17 Sept
Liverpool	H	1–3	-	24 Sept
Rotherham United	A	1–2	-	1 Oct
Stoke City	A	2–1	1	8 Oct
Chester	A	2–2	-	12 Oct (FLC)
Swansea Town	H	2–2	1	15 Oct

Opposition	Venue	Score	Goals Scored	Date (if known)
Chester	H	1–0	-	17 Oct (FLC)
Luton Town	A	1–0	-	22 Oct
Lincoln City	H	1–2	-	29 Oct
Portsmouth	A	2–1	1	5 Nov
Chesterfield	H	0–1	-	14 Nov (FLC)
Sunderland	A	1–4	-	19 Nov
Norwich City	A	2–3	1	3 Dec
Charlton Athletic	H	1–1	-	10 Dec
Ipswich Town	A	2–6	1	17 Dec
Middlesbrough	A	0–2	-	26 Dec
Scunthorpe United	H	2–1	1	31 Dec
Gillingham	A	6–2	1	3 Jan (FAC)
Sheffield United	A	1–4	-	14 Jan
Derby County	A	1–3	-	21 Jan
Southampton	A	1–0	-	28 Jan (FAC)
Bristol Rovers	H	3–2	-	4 Feb
Liverpool	A	0–5	-	11 Feb
Sheffield Wednesday	H	0–2	-	18 Feb (FAC)
Rotherham United	H	2–1	-	20 Feb
Luton Town	H	2–1	-	11 March
Middlesbrough	H	1–1	-	14 March
Charlton Athletic	A	0–2	-	18 March
Huddersfield Town	H	2–0	-	21 March
Portsmouth	H	2–1	1	25 March
Southampton	H	1–1	-	29 March
Plymouth Argyle	A	2–3	-	1 April
Southampton	A	1–1	-	3 April
Sunderland	H	0–1	-	8 April
Stoke City	H	3–1	1	10 April
Huddersfield Town	A	0–1	-	15 April
Norwich City	H	1–0	1	22 April
Lincoln City	A	0–2	-	29 April

Goals scored by Tommy Johnston for Leyton Orient in other minor competitions:

Southern Professional Floodlight Cup
1v Watford	A	13 Nov 1959

Reserves (Football Combination)
1 v Chelsea	A	26 November 1960
1 v Leicester City	A	25 February 1961

London Challenge Cup
1 v Walthamstow Avenue	H	3 October 1960

Goals scored in friendly matches:

1956–57
1 v Bromley	A	August 1956
2 v Charlton Athletic	H	26 January 1957

1957–58
2 v East Fife	H	1 March 1958

1960–61
1 v Hapoel Petach Tikva (Israel)	H	19 September 1960

(Match abandoned at half-time, pitch waterlogged)

Goals scored on tour matches:

O's in Malta 1956 (three matches played)
2 v Malta U–21s	10 May
1 v Sliema Wanderers	13 May
1 v Floriana	16 May

O's in Channel Isles May 1961 (3 matches played)
3 v Guernsey X1	

Goals scored in public trial matches:

August 1956
2 for Blues v Reds (match 1)
2 for Blues v Reds (match 2)

August 1957
1 for Blues v Reds

August 1959
1 for Blues v Reds

August 1960
1 for Reds v Blues (match 1)
1 for Blues v Reds (match 2)

Gillingham 1961–62 Division Four

Millwall	H	3–1	1	23 Sept
Aldershot	A	0–4	-	27 Sept
Mansfield Town	A	1–3	-	30 Sept
Barrow	H	3–2	1	4 Oct
Bradford City	H	3–1	-	7 Oct
Barrow	A	0–7	-	9 Oct
Carlisle United	A	2–1	-	14 Oct
Colchester United	H	2–1	1	21 Oct
Chester	A	1–1	-	28 Oct
Coventry City	A	0–2	-	4 Nov (FAC)
Southport	A	1–1	1	11 Nov
Hartlepools United	H	4–0	-	18 Nov
Oldham Athletic	A	1–1	-	9 Dec
Doncaster Rovers	A	1–2	-	19 Dec
Workington	H	4–2	1	23 Dec
Exeter City	A	3–1	-	26 Dec
Exeter City	H	2–2	-	30 Dec
Tranmere Rovers	H	0–1	-	6 Jan
York City	A	0–4	-	13 Jan
Chesterfield	H	5–1	-	20 Jan
Darlington	A	1–1	-	27 Jan
Stockport County	H	1–1	-	3 Feb

Millwall	A	0–0	-	10 Feb
Mansfield Town	H	2–2	-	17 Feb
Bradford City	A	2–5	-	24 Feb
Carlisle United	H	4–1	2	3 March
Colchester United	A	0–6	-	10 March
Chester	H	0–0	-	17 March
Tranmere Rovers	A	2–4	1	24 March
Southport	H	4–0	1	31 March
Hartlepools United	A	3–1	-	7 April
Darlington	H	2–2	1	14 April
Wrexham	A	0–3	-	20 April
Wrexham	H	2–3	-	23 April
Oldham Athletic	H	0–2	-	28 April
Rochdale	H	4–2	-	3 May

Folkestone Town 1963–64 FA Cup

Oxford United	A	0–2	-	16 Nov (First Round FA Cup)

Tommy Johnston's League and Cup goals breakdown by club and competition:
Includes all Football League, Scottish League, FA Cup, FL Cup, Scottish Cup and Welsh Cup matches only.

Goals breakdown by club

	0	*1*	*2*	*3*	*4*	
Peebles Rovers	0	1	1	4	0	
Kilmarnock	10	12	4	0	0	
Darlington	17	10	0	0	0	
Oldham Athletic	3	1	1	0	0	
Norwich City	42	19	5	0	1	
Newport County	30	25	11	2	0	
Leyton Orient	101	61	23	4	1	
Blackburn Rovers	22	10	5	1	0	
Gillingham	27	8	1	0	0	
Folkestone Town	1	0	0	0	0	
TOTALS	253	147	51	11	2	= 464

Goals breakdown by competition

Competitions	0	1	2	3	4	
Football League						
Darlington	17	10	0	0	0	
Oldham Athletic	3	1	1	0	0	
Norwich City	38	18	3	0	1	
Newport County	29	23	10	1	0	
Blackburn Rov	21	9	5	1	0	
Leyton Orient	93	59	23	4	1	
Gillingham	26	8	1	0	0	
Total	227	128	43	6	2	
Scottish League	7	9	4	0	0	
Scottish Cup	3	4	1	4	0	
Welsh Cup	0	1	1	1	0	
FA Cup	13	5	2	0	0	
FL Cup	3	0	0	0	0	
TOTAL	253	147	51	11	2	= 464

Tommy Johnston's goal breakdown

	games		goals
4 goals	2	=	8
3 goals	11	=	33
2 goals	51	=	102
1 goal	147	=	147
0 goals	253	=	0
Totals	464		290

Tommy Johnston's professional career at a glance:

Seasons	Transfer Fee £	Club/s	Apps League/Cup	Goals
1947–49*	Free	Peebles Rovers	6	15
1949–51	Free	Kilmarnock	26	20
1951–52	Free	Darlington	27	9
1951–52	500	Oldham Athletic	5	3
1952–54	2,500	Norwich City	67	33
1954–56	1,800	Newport County	68	53
1956–58**	7,500	Leyton Orient	90	71

Seasons	Transfer Fee £	Club/s	Apps League/Cup	Goals
1958–59	15,000	Blackburn Rovers	38	23
1959–61	7,500	Leyton Orient	100	52
1961–62	3,000	Gillingham	36	10
1962–64***	Free	Folkestone Town	Not available	N/A
1965–66	Free	Lytham St Annes	10	N/A

* Peebles Rovers played in the Eastern Scottish League, therefore all records for these matches were unavailable. The six matches listed were played in the Scottish Qualifying Cup.

** The transfer fee to Newport County was £5,500. Included in the deal was O's forward Mike Burgess, valued at £2,000.

*** Appearances and goals scored could not be located. As first-team coach, he played in a number of Southern League games in both the 1962–63 and 1963–64 seasons. The Folkestone Library supplied a little information but required funding to research the matter further.

Tommy Johnston's full career goalscoring record by season:

The following statistics include goals in League and FA Cup matches only, he never scored in the League Cup. The appearances include League, FA Cup and FL Cup games only.

Season	Club	Goals by comp	Apps		Total gls
1947–48	Peebles Rovers	4	Scottish Qualifying Cup	2	4
1948–48	Peebles Rovers	5	Scottish Qualifying Cup	2	5
1949–50	Peebles Rovers	6	Scottish Qualifying Cup	2	6
1949–50	Kilmarnock	13	League, 2 Scottish Cup	18	15
1950–51	Kilmarnock	4	League, 1 League Cup	8	5
1951–52	Darlington	9	League	27	10
1951–52	Oldham Athletic	3	League	5	3
1952–53	Norwich City	15	League	27	15
1953–54	Norwich City	11	League, 5 FA Cup	33	16
1954–55	Norwich City	2	League	7	2
1954–55	Newport County	26	League, 3 Welsh Cup	35	29
1955–56	Newport County	20	League, 1 FA Cup, 3 Welsh Cup	33	24
1955–56	Leyton Orient	8	League	15	8
1956–57	Leyton Orient	27	League	43	27
1957–58	Leyton Orient	35	League, 1 FA Cup	32	36

1957–58	Blackburn Rovers	8	League	11	8
1958–59	Blackburn Rovers	14	League, 1 FA Cup	27	15
1958–59	Leyton Orient	10	League	14	10
1959–60	Leyton Orient	25	League	40	25
1960–61	Leyton Orient	16	League, 1 FA Cup	46	17
1961–62	Gillingham	10	League	36	10
1963–64	Folkestone Town			1	0
TOTALS				464	290

Tommy Johnston's appearances and goals by competition:

Competition	Apps	Goals
Leagues		
Scottish	20	18
English	409	239
Major Cups		
Scottish	12	18
Welsh	3	6
FA Cup	20	9
FL Cup	3	-
Totals	464	290

Discrepancy in the number of League goals scored by Tommy Johnston:
In the 1981 (first edition) book by Barry Hugman entitled *Football Players Records* it shows on p197 that Tommy Johnston scored 119 League goals for Orient with a career total of 237 League goals. However, the totals shown in this book are incorrect. The correct totals are shown below, on the left, under the authors' verified totals.

Club	Authors' verified totals	Barry Hugman's book (1981 edition) totals
Darlington	9	9
Oldham Athletic	3	3
Norwich City	28	28

Newport County	46	46
Leyton Orient	121	119
Blackburn Rovers	22	22
Gillingham	10	10
TOTALS	239	237

The above totals listed on the right show a discrepancy with the goals scored for Leyton Orient. Below are Tommy Johnston's verified seasonal League goals that he scored for Orient.

Season	League Goals Scored
1955–56	8
1956–57	27
1957–58	35
1958–59	10
1959–60	25
1960–61	16
TOTALS	121

Breakdown of appearances and goals scored by Tommy Johnston against all clubs he played against:

English and Scottish League, Scottish Cup, Welsh Cup, FA Cup and FL Cup games only.

Club	Apps	Goals
A		
Abergavenny	1	2
Accrington Stanley	2	0
Airdrieonians	2	0
Albion Rovers	1	1
Aldershot	9	4
Alloa Athletic	2	3
Arbroath	2	3
Arsenal	2	2
Aston Villa	3	2
Ayr United	2	1

B

Babcock & Wilcox	1	2
Barnsley	5	8
Barrow	3	1
Barry Town	1	3
Birmingham City	1	0
Blackburn Rovers	3	3
Blackpool	2	0
Bolton Wanderers	1	0
Bournemouth	5	2
Bradford City	2	0
Brentford	4	2
Brighton & Hove Albion	13	7
Bristol City	11	9
Bristol Rovers	7	1
Burnley	2	0
Bury	2	3

C

Cardiff City	8	9
Carlisle United	4	2
Charlton Athletic	7	4
Chelsea	3	0
Chester	5	1
Chesterfield	2	0
Colchester United	7	2
Coldstream	1	3
Coventry City	5	1
Crewe Alexandra	2	0
Crystal Palace	8	3

D

Darlington	2	1
Derby County	4	2
Doncaster Rovers	7	5

Dumbarton	2	1
Dundee United	1	0
Dunfermline Athletic	3	4
Duns	1	3

E

East Stirlingshire	3	6
Edinburgh City	1	1
Everton	1	0
Exeter City	8	4

F

Forfar Athletic	1	0
Fulham	5	1

G

Gateshead	1	1
Gillingham	7	7
Grimsby Town	8	9

H

Hamilton Academical	1	2
Hartlepools United	3	1
Hastings United	1	1
Huddersfield Town	7	2
Hull City	2	3

I

Ipswich Town	10	6

L

Leeds United	3	1
Leicester City	5	3
Leyton Orient	7	9
Lincoln City	10	2

Liverpool	10	3
Luton Town	3	1

M

Manchester City	1	1
Manchester United	1	0
Mansfield Town	4	3
Middlesbrough	9	3
Millwall	9	5
Morton	1	0

N

Newcastle United	2	5
Newport County	3	1
Northampton Town	6	2
Norwich City	3	3
Nottingham Forest	2	2
Notts County	4	4

O

Oldham Athletic	4	1
Oxford United	1	0

P

Plymouth Argyle	3	0
Portsmouth	5	3
Port Vale	2	2

Q

Queens Park	2	2
Queens Park Rangers	7	4

R

Reading	5	6
Rochdale	3	1
Rotherham United	9	10

S

St Johnstone	2	1
Scunthorpe United	6	5
Sheffield United	8	5
Sheffield Wednesday	1	0
Shrewsbury Town	8	8
Southampton	10	1
Southend United	4	1
Southport	4	2
Stenhousemuir	1	1
Stirling Albion	2	1
Stockport County	3	1
Stoke City	9	9
Sunderland	5	2
Swansea Town	6	5
Swindon Town	6	5

T

Tonbridge	2	0
Torquay United	8	5
Tottenham Hotspur	2	2
Tranmere Rovers	4	2

W

Walsall	8	7
Watford	5	2
West Bromwich Albion	1	1
West Ham United	5	2
Wolverhampton Wand	2	0
Workington	3	1
Wrexham	2	0

Y

York City	3	0
TOTALS	464	290

Authors' Note: Only matches in the Football League, Scottish League and all major cup competitions in England, Scotland and Wales are included. Minor cup matches, friendlies, reserve or tour matches are not.

Rotherham United top the list, but Leyton Orient are second with nine goals scored against them by Johnston from just seven matches.

The above statistics show that Tommy Johnston scored the most goals against Rotherham United, with 10 goals from nine matches, bolstered by the four goals he scored against them for Orient in December 1957. He scored nine goals against Leyton Orient from just seven matches.

Other beleaguered opposition include: Cardiff City (nine goals from eight matches) Stoke City (nine goals from nine matches) and Bristol City (nine goals from 11 matches).

The clubs he played against most were Brighton & Hove Albion (13 games with seven goals scored) and Bristol City (11 matches, nine goals scored).

Tommy Johnston played against 114 different teams throughout his career in English and Scottish League and major Cup competitions – he scored against 92 different teams and failed to score against 22 different teams, he played in 464 League and senior cup matches, and he failed to score in 253 of them.

League and Cup goals scored against Leyton Orient by Johnston:
Tommy played against Leyton Orient in seven matches and failed to score in just one of them. His record against Orient reads:

1953–54
2 for Norwich City v O's	H (at Carrow Road)	3 April 1954

1954–55
1 for Newport County v O's	A (at Brisbane Road)	17 March 1955
1 for Newport County v O's	H (at Newport)	30 April 1955 (a penalty kick)

1955–56
3 for Newport County v O's	H (at Newport)	8 October 1955
1 for Newport County v O's	A (at Leyton)	18 February 1956

1957–58
0 for Blackburn Rovers v O's	H (at Ewood Park)	19 April 1958

(It should be noted that Johnston made three goals for Roy Vernon and one for Ally McLeod in this match)

1958–59
1 for Blackburn Rovers v O's	H (at Ewood Park)	10 January 1959

FA Cup tie.

Tommy Johnston also scored from a penalty kick against O's for an ex-Leyton Orient XI in Phil White's testimonial match on 21 April 1964, held at Leyton Stadium.